THE IBIZA ADVENTURE: A TRAVEL PREPARATION GUIDE

SHONDA WILLIAMS

Table of Contents

Introduction   **9**

Chapter 1 • Welcome to Ibiza   **11**

Overview of Ibiza   11

Why Visit Ibiza?   13

Chapter 2 • Planning Your Trip   **15**

Best Time to Visit Ibiza   15

Visa Requirements and Travel Documents   18

Airports and Airlines   21

Currency and Money Matters   24

Transportation in Ibiza   28

Accommodation Options   30

Chapter 3 • Ibizan Culture and Etiquette   **35**

Ibizan Language and Basic Phrases   35

Cultural Norms and Customs   38

Dining Etiquette   42

Dress Code and Fashion in Ibiza   45

Festivals and Celebrations   47

Chapter 4 • Exploring Ibiza's Regions   **53**

Ibiza Town and South Coast   53

Dalt Vila: the old town   55

La Marina: the harbour district   58

Talamanca: the nearest beach   59

Playa d'en Bossa: the party hotspot   60

Ses Salines: the nature reserve and beach   61

Sa Caleta: the Phoenician site and cove   63

Es Cavallet: the nudist beach   65

Recommendations for Accommodation   67

Recommendations for Restaurants   69

San Antonio and West Coast   71

San Antonio: the sunset strip and nightlife   73

Cala Salada: the scenic beach   75

Cala Bassa: the chic beach club   77

Cala Conta: the stunning views and turquoise waters   79

Cala Tarida: the family-friendly resort   80

Es Vedrà: the mysterious island   81

Recommendations for Accommodation   84

Recommendations for Restaurants   86

Santa Eulàlia and East Coast   88

Santa Eulàlia: the relaxed town and promenade 90

Puig de Missa: the hilltop church and museum 93

Es Canar: the hippy market and resort   95

Cala Nova: the surfers' beach   96

Cala Llenya: the pine-fringed cove   97

Cala Mastella: the rustic beach and restaurant 98

Recommendations for Accommodation   100

Recommendations for Restaurants   103

North Coast and Interior   105

Sant Joan: the sleepy village   107

Portinatx: the secluded bay and lighthouse   108

Sant Miquel: the cave and beach   109

Sant Llorenç: the rural charm   110

Santa Gertrudis: the gastronomic hub   111

Sant Rafel: the pottery town   114

Recommendations for Accommodation 115
Recommendations for Restaurants 117
Formentera 120
How to get there and around 122
La Savina: the port and salt flats 126
Sant Francesc: the capital and church square 128
Illetes: the Caribbean-like beach 130
Es Pujols: the main tourist resort 132
La Mola: the lighthouse and market 134
Recommendations for Accommodation 136
Recommendations for Restaurants 139

Chapter 5 • Ibiza Cuisine and Food Experiences 143
Introduction to Ibiza Cuisine 143
Regional Specialties 145
Famous Ibiza Dishes 147
Wine and Food Pairing 150
Culinary Experiences and Cooking Classes 151

Chapter 6 • Outdoor Activities and Nature 155
Clubbing in Ibiza 155
Hiking and Trekking in Ibiza 157
Cycling in Ibiza 160
Watersports in Ibiza 163
Skiing in Ibiza 166
Exploring National Parks 170
Beaches and Coastal Escapes 173

Chapter 7 • Shopping in Ibiza 177
Fashion and Luxury Shopping 177
Local Markets and Souvenirs 179

Artisan Crafts and Workshops 182

Antique and Vintage Shopping 184

Wellness: Spas, Retreats, and Yoga 187

Chapter 8 • Practical Information **191**

Health and Safety Tips 191

Emergency Contacts 196

Communication and Internet Access 200

Chapter 9 • Recommended Itineraries **207**

3 Days in Ibiza for Party Lovers 207

3 Days in Ibiza for Nature Lovers 211

3 Days in Ibiza for Food Lovers 216

3 Days in Ibiza for Culture Lovers 221

3 Days in Ibiza for Couples 225

Chapter 10 • Travelling with Children **231**

Family-Friendly Attractions 231

Child-Friendly Accommodation 234

Chapter 11 • Travelling on a Budget **241**

Budget-Friendly Accommodation 241

Cheap Eats and Local Food 244

Free and Affordable Attractions 248

Transportation Tips for Saving Money 253

Conclusion **257**

Introduction

Welcome to Ibiza, the dazzling island that will enchant you with its natural beauty, cultural heritage, and legendary nightlife. Ibiza is one of the four Balearic Islands of Spain, located in the western Mediterranean Sea. It has a rich history that dates back to ancient times when it was inhabited by the Phoenicians, the Carthaginians, the Romans, the Arabs, and the Catalans. You can explore the traces of these civilizations in the archaeological sites, museums, and monuments that dot the island, especially in the stunning old town of Dalt Vila, a UNESCO World Heritage Site.

Ibiza is also famous for its natural wonders, such as its

pristine beaches, rugged cliffs, pine forests, salt flats, and marine reserves. You can enjoy the sun and the sea in more than 80 coves and bays that offer crystal-clear water and white sand. You can also discover the hidden gems of the island by hiking, cycling, kayaking, diving, or snorkelling. And don't miss the chance to visit Formentera, the neighbouring island that boasts some of the most spectacular beaches in the Mediterranean.

But Ibiza is not only about nature and culture. It is also about fun and entertainment. Ibiza is known as the world's clubbing capital, where you can dance until dawn to the beats of the best DJs in venues like Pacha, Amnesia, and Ushuaïa. You can also enjoy the sunset with a cocktail at one of the many beach bars and chill-out spots that line the coast or you can shop at the hippy markets and boutiques that sell local crafts and clothes.

Ibiza is an island that will surprise you with its charm. It is a place where you can find your rhythm and style. It is an island that will make you fall in love with its magic and spirit. It is an island that awaits you.

Chapter 1 • Welcome to Ibiza

Overview of Ibiza

Ibiza is a Spanish island in the Mediterranean Sea, located about 150 kilometres (93 miles) from the city of Valencia. It is the third largest of the Balearic Islands, after Mallorca and Menorca. Ibiza is famous for its nightlife, beaches, and natural beauty, but it also has a rich cultural heritage that dates back to ancient times. Below are some of the main attractions and activities that you can enjoy on this enchanting island.

You can explore the Unesco-listed Dalt Vila, the historic centre of Ibiza Town, where you can admire the medieval walls, the Gothic cathedral, the castle, and the archaeological museum. Dalt Vila was founded by the Phoenicians in the 7th century BC and later occupied by the Carthaginians, Romans, Moors, and Catalans .

You can relax on the stunning beaches and coves that dot the island's coastline, such as Cala Bassa, Es Vedrà, Cala Comte, Cala d'Hort, and Las Salinas. You can swim, snorkel, surf, kayak, or sail in the clear blue waters, or simply soak up the sun and the views.

You can experience the nightlife and club scene that Ibiza is famous for. You can dance until dawn at some of the world's best clubs, such as Pacha, Amnesia, Ushuaïa, Privilege, and DC10. You can also enjoy live music, bars, restaurants, and street performers in the lively towns of San Antonio and Santa Eulalia .

You can discover the rural charm and tranquility of the island's north coast, where you can find pine-covered hills, white-washed villages, and secluded coves. You can visit Sant Joan de Labritja, Portinatx, Sant Mateu d'Aubarca, Santa Agnès de Corona, and other picturesque places. You can also go horseback riding with Ibiza Horse Valley, a sanctuary for rescued horses.

You can learn about the island's history at various museums and galleries. You can see contemporary art at the Museu d'Art Contemporani d'Eivissa, ancient artefacts at the Necròpolis Puig des Molins, or traditional crafts at the Museu Etnològic d'Eivissa. You can also admire the architecture and art of the island's churches and cathedrals.

You can enjoy the local cuisine and gastronomy of Ibiza, which reflects its Mediterranean and multicultural influences. You can taste typical dishes such as sofrit pagès (a stew of meat and potatoes), bullit de peix (a fish soup with rice), flaó (a cheese and mint tart), or greixonera (a pudding made with bread and eggs). You can also try some of the island's specialties such as sobrasada (a cured sausage), ensaimada (a spiral-shaped pastry), or hierbas ibicencas (an anise-flavoured liqueur).

Ibiza is a destination that offers something for everyone, be it adventure, relaxation, culture, or fun. It is a place where you can discover new experiences and create unforgettable memories. Ibiza is more than just an island; it is a state of mind.

Why Visit Ibiza?

Below are some of the reasons why you should visit this amazing island:

Clubbing: Ibiza is the ultimate party destination, where you can enjoy some of the best nightlife and electronic dance music in the world. Ibiza is a place where you can have fun and make memories that will last a lifetime.

Beaches: Ibiza has more than 80 beaches and coves to choose from, each with its charm and character. You can find everything from Playa d'en Bossa and San Antonio to scenic coves like Cala Conta and Cala Tarida.

Culture: Ibiza has a diverse history that goes back to ancient times when it was inhabited by the Phoenicians, the Carthaginians, the Romans, the Arabs, and the Catalans. You can also discover the island's traditions and customs, such as its cuisine, its crafts, its festivals, and its music.

Nature: Ibiza is not only about the sun and sea. It is also about nature and beauty. You can see some of the island's iconic sights, such as the mysterious island of Es Vedrà or the ancient cave of Cova de Can Marçà. You can also enjoy a wellness break at one of the many spas, yoga studios, or retreats that helps you relax and rejunevate.

Chapter 2 • Planning Your Trip

Best Time to Visit Ibiza

The best time to visit Ibiza depends on what you are looking for in your trip. Ibiza is a destination that offers different experiences throughout the year, from the peak of the party season in summer to the tranquillity of the low season in winter. Below are some factors to consider when planning your visit:

Weather: Ibiza has a hot semi-arid climate, with mild winters and hot summers. The average annual temperature is 18.3 °C (65 °F), but it can vary from 10 °C (50 °F) in January to 29 °C (84 °F) in August. The island enjoys plenty of sunshine, with more than 300 sunny days per year. The sea temperature is also pleasant, ranging from 15 °C (59 °F) in February to 26 °C (79 °F) in August. The best time to visit Ibiza for the weather is from May to October when you can enjoy warm and sunny days and cool nights.

Nightlife: Ibiza is famous for its nightlife which attracts millions of tourists every year. The island has some of the best clubs and beach bars in the world, where you can see the most renowned DJs perform. The nightlife season usually starts in late May with the opening parties and ends in early October with the closing parties. The peak of the nightlife season is from June to September when most of the clubs and bars are open and crowded. The best time to visit Ibiza for nightlife is from June to September when you can experience the full vibe and energy of the island.

Festivals: Ibiza hosts several festivals and events throughout the year, celebrating its culture, music, art, and gastronomy. Some of the most popular festivals are:

International Music Summit (May): A three-day conference and festival that brings together industry leaders, artists, and fans of electronic music.

Moda Adlib Fashion Show (May): A showcase of local designers and their creations inspired by the island's bohemian style.

Ibiza Rocks (June): A series of live concerts featuring rock, indie, and alternative bands at the Ibiza Rocks Hotel.

Festes de la Terra (August): A celebration of the patron saints of Ibiza Town and Formentera, with parades, fireworks, concerts, and cultural activities.

Ibiza Jazz Festival (September): A three-day event that features local and international jazz musicians at various venues in Dalt Vila.

Ibiza Light Festival (October): A two-night event that transforms the streets and buildings of Ibiza Town into a spectacle of light and sound art.

Prices: Ibiza is not a cheap destination, especially during the high season. The prices of flights, hotels, restaurants, clubs, and attractions can be very high from June to September when the demand is highest. You can expect to pay more than double for accommodation and entrance fees than in the low season. The best time to visit Ibiza for prices is from November to April when you can find lower rates and deals on flights and hotels. However, you should also consider that some services and attractions may be closed or have reduced hours during this period.

Crowds: Ibiza is a very popular destination, especially among young people who come for the nightlife and the beaches. The island can get very crowded from June to September when most of the tourists arrive. You may have to deal with long queues, traffic jams, noise, and pollution during this time. The best time to visit Ibiza for crowds is in May or October, when you can still enjoy good weather and nightlife, but with fewer people around. You can also visit from November to April, when you can have more peace, but with fewer options for entertainment.

In conclusion, there is no one best time to visit Ibiza, as it depends on your preferences and expectations. You can choose to visit during the summer if you want to enjoy the hottest weather and the liveliest nightlife, or during the winter if you want to save money and avoid crowds. You can also opt for the shoulder seasons if you want a balance between both options. Whatever you decide, Ibiza will offer you an unforgettable experience that will make you want to come back again.

Visa Requirements and Travel Documents

Before you pack your bags and head to Ibiza, you need to make sure you have the right documents to enter Spain, the country that Ibiza belongs to. Depending on your nationality and the purpose and duration of your visit, you may need a passport, a visa, or both. Below are some of the main things you need to know:

Passport: A passport is a travel document that proves your identity and nationality. You need a passport to enter Spain if you are not a citizen of the European Union (EU), the European Economic Area (EEA), or Switzerland. Your passport must be valid for at least six months beyond your planned departure date from Spain and must have been issued within the past 10 years. It must also have at least two blank pages for visa stamps.

National ID card: A national ID card is a document that proves your identity and nationality within the EU, the EEA, or Switzerland. You can use a national ID card to enter Spain instead of a passport if you are a citizen of one of these countries. Your national ID card must be valid for the duration of your stay in Spain.

Visa: A visa is a document that grants you permission to enter, stay, or transit through a country for a specific period and purpose. You need a visa to enter Spain if you are not a citizen of the EU, the EEA, Switzerland, or one of the 62 countries that have a visa-free agreement with Spain. You can check if you need a visa on the website of the Spanish Ministry of Foreign Affairs. The type of visa you need depends on your reason and the length of your visit. The most common types are:

Schengen visa: A Schengen visa allows you to travel

within the 26 countries that form part of the Schengen Area, including Spain, for up to 90 days within 180 days. You can apply for a Schengen visa at the Spanish embassy or consulate in your country of residence. You will need to fill out an application form, provide two recent passport-sized photos, and show proof of travel insurance, flight reservations, accommodation bookings, financial means, and any other documents that support your purpose of visit. You will also need to pay a visa fee and attend an interview.

National visa: A national visa allows you to stay in Spain for more than 90 days for reasons such as work, study, family reunification, or residence. You can apply for a national visa at the Spanish embassy or consulate in your country of residence. You will need to fill out an application form, provide two recent passport-sized photos, and show proof of travel insurance, flight reservations, accommodation bookings, financial means, and any other documents that support your purpose of visit. You will also need to pay a visa fee and attend an interview.

It is important to apply for your visa well in advance of your trip, as it may take several weeks or months to process your application. You should also check the validity and expiry date of your visa before you travel, as well as any restrictions or conditions that apply to it.

Remember that having a valid passport and visa does not guarantee your entry into Spain. You may still be asked by the immigration officers to show additional documents or evidence of your travel plans, such as return tickets, hotel reservations, invitation letters, etc. You should also respect the rules and regulations of Spain during your stay and leave before your visa expires.

We hope this information helps you prepare for your trip to Ibiza. If you have any questions or doubts about your visa requirements and travel documents, we recommend contacting the Spanish embassy or consulate in your country or visiting the official websites of the Spanish authorities. We wish you a safe and enjoyable journey!

Airports and Airlines

If you are planning to fly to Ibiza, you need to know about the airports and airlines that serve the island.

Below are some of the main things you need to know:

Ibiza Airport: Ibiza Airport (IBZ) is the only airport on the island, located about 7 km (4 miles) southwest of Ibiza Town. It is a small but busy airport, especially in summer, when it handles more than 8 million passengers per year. The airport has one terminal building, divided into two areas: arrivals and departures. The airport offers various services and facilities, such as shops, restaurants, ATMs, car rental offices, taxi ranks, bus stops, and parking lots. You can also find a permanent exhibition of archaeological finds from the area where the airport is located.

Getting to and from the airport: There are several options to get to and from the airport, depending on your budget and preference. You can take a taxi, which costs around 15-20 euros to Ibiza Town or San Antonio, which takes about 15-20 minutes. You can also take a bus, which costs around 4 euros and runs every 20 minutes to Ibiza Town or every hour to San Antonio. The bus journey takes about 30 minutes to either destination. You can also rent a car, which gives you more flexibility and freedom to explore the island. You can find several car rental companies at the airport, such as Avis, Europcar, Hertz, or Sixt.

Airlines and destinations: Ibiza Airport is connected to more than 90 destinations in Europe and Africa, operated by more than 40 airlines. Some of the most popular airlines and destinations are:

Ryanair: The low-cost carrier flies to Ibiza from several cities in the UK, such as London, Manchester, Birmingham, Edinburgh, and Glasgow. It also flies from other European cities, such as Barcelona, Madrid, Rome, Milan, Berlin, and Paris.

Vueling: The Spanish low-cost carrier flies to Ibiza from several cities in Spain, such as Barcelona, Madrid, Valencia, Bilbao, or Seville. It also flies from other European cities, such as London, Amsterdam, Paris, Rome, or Brussels.

British Airways: The flag carrier of the UK flies to Ibiza from London Heathrow or London City airports.

EasyJet: The low-cost carrier flies to Ibiza from several cities in the UK, such as London Gatwick or Luton airports.

TUI Airways: The charter airline flies to Ibiza from several cities in the UK and Ireland, such as London Gatwick or Stansted airports.

Iberia Express: The low-cost subsidiary of Iberia flies to Ibiza from Madrid or Palma de Mallorca airports.

Jet2.com: The low-cost carrier flies to Ibiza from several cities in the UK, such as Leeds Bradford and Manchester airports.

You can find more information about the airlines and destinations on the official website of Ibiza Airport or online flight search engines. You can also compare prices and book your flights online.

We hope this information helps you plan your trip to Ibiza. If you have any questions or doubts about the airports and airlines that serve the island, we recommend contacting your airline or travel agent for more details. We wish you a safe and enjoyable flight!

Currency and Money Matters

One of the most important things to consider when planning your trip to Ibiza is how to manage your money. You need to know what currency to use, how to exchange it, how to access it, and how much to budget for your expenses. Below are some of the main things you need to know:

Currency: The official currency in Ibiza is the Euro (EUR), which is divided into 100 cents. You can find coins of 1, 2, 5, 10, 20, 50 cents, and 1 and 2 euros. You can also find banknotes of 5, 10, 20, 50, 100, 200, and 500 euros. The euro is the same currency used in most of the European Union countries, so you don't need to exchange it if you are travelling from or to another EU country.

Exchange: If you need to exchange your currency for euros, you have several options. You can do it before you travel at your local bank or currency exchange office, but make sure you compare the rates and fees to get the best deal. You can also do it at the airport or your destination, but be aware that the rates and fees may be higher than elsewhere. You can also use ATMs or credit cards to withdraw or pay in euros, but check with your bank or card provider about the charges and limits that apply.

Access: There are plenty of ATMs in Ibiza, especially in the main towns and tourist areas. You can use them to withdraw cash in euros with your debit or credit card, but remember to check the fees and exchange rates that apply. You can also use your credit or debit card to pay for goods and services in most places, such as shops, restaurants, hotels, or clubs. However, some small businesses or rural areas may only accept cash or have a minimum amount for card payments. It is always advisable to carry some cash with you for emergencies or small purchases.

Budget: Ibiza is not a cheap destination, especially during the high season from June to September. The prices of accommodation, food, drinks, transport, and entertainment can be very high during this time. You can expect to spend between 60 and 90 euros per day as a backpacker, depending on your lifestyle and preferences. You can spend more or less depending on your choices of accommodation, food, activities, and nightlife. Below are some examples of average prices in Ibiza:

Accommodation: A dorm bed in a hostel can cost between 15 and 30 euros per night. A private room in a budget hotel can cost between 40 and 80 euros per night. A mid-range hotel room can cost between 80 and 150 euros per night. A luxury hotel room can cost between 150 and 300 euros per night or more.

Food: A meal in an inexpensive restaurant can cost between 7 and 13 euros. A meal in a mid-range restaurant can cost between 15 and 25 euros. A meal in a high-end restaurant can cost between 30 and 50 euros or more. A fast-food meal can cost between 5 and 10 euros. A coffee can cost between 1 and 2 euros. A beer can cost between 2 and 4 euros. A bottle of water can cost between 0.5 and 1 euro.

Transport: A bus ticket can cost between 1.5 and 3 euros depending on the distance. A taxi ride can cost between 10 and 20 euros depending on the distance and time of day. A car rental can cost between 30 and 60 euros per day plus fuel and insurance.

Activities: A ticket to a museum or a historical site can cost between 2 and 10 euros depending on the place. A ticket to a boat trip or a water sport activity can cost between 20 and 50 euros depending on the type and duration. A ticket to a club or a beach bar can cost between 20 and 50 euros depending on the venue and the event.

Tips: Tipping is not mandatory in Ibiza, but it is appreciated as a sign of gratitude for good service. You can tip around 10% of the bill in restaurants or bars if you are satisfied with the service. You can also tip taxi drivers, hotel staff, tour guides, or other service providers if you wish.

We hope this information helps you plan your money matters for your trip to Ibiza. If you have any questions or doubts about your currency and money matters, we recommend contacting your bank or travel agent for more details. We wish you a happy and hassle-free holiday!

Transportation in Ibiza

Ibiza is a small island that can be easily explored by different means of transportation. Depending on your budget, preference, and destination, you can choose from various options to get around the island. Below are some of the main things you need to know:

Car: Renting a car is the best way to enjoy the freedom and flexibility to discover the island at your own pace. You can find many car rental companies at the airport or in the main towns, offering competitive rates and a wide range of vehicles. You can also bring your car by ferry from mainland Spain or other Balearic Islands. Driving in Ibiza is generally easy and safe, as the roads are well-maintained and signposted. However, you should be aware of some potential challenges, such as traffic jams, parking difficulties, or narrow roads in rural areas. You should also respect the speed limits, traffic rules, and parking regulations, as there are fines for violations.

Bus: Taking the bus is a cheap and convenient way to get around the island, especially if you don't have a car or want to avoid driving. There are more than 40 bus lines that cover most of the island, connecting the main towns, resorts, beaches, and attractions. The buses are comfortable and air-conditioned and run frequently during the high season from June to September. However, they may have reduced schedules or stop operating during the low season from October to May. You can check the timetables, routes, and fares on the official website of Ibiza Bus or at the bus stations.

Taxi: Taking a taxi is a fast and easy way to get around the island at any time of the day or night. You can find taxi ranks at the airport, in the main towns, or near popular places. You can also call a taxi by phone or use an app like Ibiza Taxi or Taxi Click. The taxis are metered and have fixed rates for certain destinations, such as the airport or the port. You can expect to pay between 10 and 20 euros for a short ride, depending on the distance and time of day. You can also tip the driver if you are satisfied with the service.

Boat: Taking a boat is a fun and scenic way to get around the island or to visit other islands nearby. You can find boat trips and ferry rides that connect certain areas to different coves or beaches. For example, you can take a boat from Ibiza Town to Formentera, a smaller island that has some of the most beautiful beaches in the Mediterranean. You can also take a boat from San Antonio to Cala Bassa or Cala Conta, two stunning coves with clear water and views of small islands. You can check the timetables, routes, and fares on the official websites of Ibiza Boat Service or Aquabus Ferry Boats.

We hope this information helps you plan your transportation in Ibiza. If you have any questions or doubts about your transportation in Ibiza, we recommend contacting your travel agent or hotel for more details. We wish you a happy and hassle-free holiday!

Accommodation Options

Ibiza is a popular destination that offers a wide range of accommodation options to suit different tastes, budgets, and needs. Below are some of the main things you need to know:

Apartments: Renting an apartment is a great option if you want to enjoy more space, privacy, and flexibility. You can find apartments of various sizes, styles, and locations on the island, from the old town of Ibiza to the lively resorts of San Antonio or Playa den Bossa. You can also find apartments with amenities such as a kitchen, balcony, pool, or sea view. You can book apartments online through platforms such as Airbnb, Booking.com, or HomeAway, or through local agencies such as Ibiza Spotlight or Ibiza House Renting. The prices vary depending on the season, location, and quality of the apartment, but you can expect to pay between 40 and 200 euros per night for a standard apartment.

Villas: Renting a villa is a perfect option if you want to enjoy more luxury, comfort, and exclusivity. You can find villas of various sizes, styles, and locations on the island, from the countryside to the coast. You can also find villas with amenities such as a garden, pool, barbecue, or jacuzzi. You can book villas online through platforms such as Airbnb, Booking.com, or HomeAway, or through local agencies such as Ibiza Villas or Ibiza Luxury Villas. The prices vary depending on the season, location, and quality of the villa, but you can expect to pay between 200 and 1000 euros per night for a standard villa.

Hotels: Staying in a hotel is a convenient option if you want to enjoy more services, facilities, and security. You can find hotels of various categories, styles, and locations on the island, from budget to luxury. You can also find hotels with amenities such as restaurants, bars, spas, gyms, or pools. You can book hotels online through platforms such as Booking.com, Expedia, or Tripadvisor, or directly through the hotel's website. The prices vary depending on the season, location, and quality of the hotel, but you can expect to pay between 50 and 300 euros per night for a standard hotel.

Boutique hotels: Staying in a boutique hotel is a charming option if you want to enjoy more personality, design, and atmosphere. You can find boutique hotels of various categories, styles, and locations on the island, from urban to rural. You can also find boutique hotels with amenities such as a terrace, art gallery, library, or yoga studio. You can book boutique hotels online through platforms such as Booking.com, Expedia, or Tripadvisor, or directly through the hotel's website. The prices vary depending on the season, location, and quality of the boutique hotel, but you can expect to pay between 100 and 400 euros per night for a standard boutique hotel.

Campsites: Staying in a campsite is a cheap and fun option if you want to enjoy more nature and adventure.

You can find campsites of various sizes and locations on the island, from near the beach to in the forest. You can also find campsites with amenities such as showers, toilets, kitchens, bars, or playgrounds. You can book campsites online through platforms such as Pitchup.com, Camping.info, or Campingsonline.com, or directly through the campsite's website. The prices vary depending on the season, location, and quality of the campsite, but you can expect to pay between 10 and 30 euros per night for a standard campsite.

We hope this information helps you plan your accommodation options in Ibiza. We wish you a happy and comfortable stay!

Chapter 3 • Ibizan Culture and Etiquette

Ibizan Language and Basic Phrases

Ibiza is a multicultural and multilingual island, where you can hear different languages spoken by locals and visitors alike. However, the two official languages of Ibiza are Spanish and Catalan, or more specifically, Eivissenc, a dialect of Catalan that is unique to the island. If you want to communicate with the locals and learn more about their culture and history, it is useful to know some basic phrases and pronunciations of Ibiza. Below are some of the main things you need to know:

Spanish: Spanish is the most widely spoken language on the island, as it is the common language of education, media, and administration. It is also the language that most tourists use to communicate with the locals. Spanish is a Romance language that derives from Latin and has many similarities with other languages such as French, Italian, or Portuguese. Spanish uses the Latin alphabet and has 27 letters, including ñ (pronounced like ny in the canyon) and ll (pronounced like y in yes). Spanish is also a phonetic language, which means that each letter has a fixed sound and words are pronounced as they are written. Some basic phrases in Spanish are:

Hello: Hola (OH-lah)

Goodbye: Adiós (ah-DYOS)

Please: Por favour (por fah-VOR)

Thank you: Gracias (GRAH-syahs)

You're welcome: De nada (deh NAH-dah)

Excuse me: Perdón (pehr-DON)

How are you?: ¿Qué tal? (keh TAL)

I'm fine: Estoy bien (ehs-TOY byen)

Do you speak English?: ¿Habla inglés? (AH-blah een-GLEHS)

I don't understand: No entiendo (noh ehn-TYEN-doh)

How much is it?: ¿Cuánto cuesta? (KWAHN-toh KWEH-stash)

Where is...?: ¿Dónde está...? (DON-deh ehs-TAH)

Open: Abierto (ah-BYER-toh)

Closed: Cerrado (seh-RAH-doh)

Catalan/Eivissenc: Catalan is the co-official language of Ibiza, along with Spanish, and it is the native language of many locals. It is also the language of culture, identity, and tradition on the island. Catalan is a Romance language that derives from Latin and has many similarities with other languages such as French, Italian, or Spanish. Catalan uses the Latin alphabet and has 26 letters, plus ç (pronounced like s in sun) and l·l (pronounced like ly in million). Catalan also has some sounds that are different from Spanish, such as x (pronounced like sh in a shoe), j (pronounced like zh in measure), or ny (pronounced like gn in lasagna). Eivissenc is a dialect of Catalan that is spoken only in Ibiza and Formentera, and it has some variations in vocabulary, grammar, and pronunciation from standard Catalan. Some basic phrases in Eivissenc are:

Hello: Hola (OH-lah)

Goodbye: Adéu (ah-DEH-oo)

Please: Si us plau (see oos PLOW)

Thank you: Gràcies (GRAH-syes)

You're welcome: De res (deh REHS)

Excuse me: Perdó/Perdoni (pperDOH/pperDOH-nee)

How are you?: Com estàs?/Com anam? (kohm ehs-TAHS/kohm ah-NAHM)

I'm fine: Estic bé/Anam bé (ehs-TEEK beh/ah-NAHM beh)

Do you speak English?: Parles anglès?/Parla anglès? (PAHR-less ahn-GLEHS/PAHR-lah ahn-GLEHS)

I don't understand: No sentence/No entengué (noh ehn-TENK/noh ehn-then-GWEH)

How much is it?: Quant costa?/Quant val? (KWAHN kohs-TAH/KWAHN Bahl

Where is...?: On és...?/On està...? (ohn EHS/ohn ehs-TAH)

Open: Obert (oh-BEHR)

Closed: Tancat (tahn-KAHT)

We hope this information helps you learn some Ibiza language and basic phrases. We wish you a happy and enjoyable holiday!

Cultural Norms and Customs

Ibiza is a dynamic island, where you can experience different cultures, traditions, and lifestyles. However, there are also some common norms and customs that you should be aware of and respect when visiting the island. Below are some of the main things you need to know:

Greetings: The typical greeting in Ibiza is a handshake, accompanied by a smile and eye contact. However, if you are familiar with someone, you can also greet them with a kiss on each cheek, starting from the left. This applies to both men and women, although men may also hug each other if they are close friends or relatives. When greeting a group of people, it is polite to greet each person individually, rather than waving or saying hello to everyone at once.

Conversation: The locals in Ibiza are friendly and sociable, and they enjoy having conversations with visitors. They are usually open and expressive, and they may use gestures and facial expressions to emphasize their points. They are also interested in learning about other cultures and perspectives, but they may also be proud and passionate about their own. Some topics that are safe and popular to talk about are sports, music, art, food, travel, or local attractions. Some topics that are best to avoid or be careful with are politics, religion, personal issues, or negative stereotypes.

Etiquette: The locals in Ibiza are generally relaxed and informal, but they also appreciate good manners and respect. Some basic etiquette rules to follow are:

Dress appropriately for the occasion and the place. While casual wear is acceptable for most situations, some places such as churches, museums, or upscale restaurants may require more formal or modest attire.

Avoid wearing beachwear or revealing clothing outside the beach or pool areas.

Be punctual for appointments or meetings, but do not expect the same from the locals. They may have a more flexible attitude towards time and may arrive late or change plans without notice. This is not a sign of disrespect or rudeness, but rather a reflection of their laid-back lifestyle.

Be courteous and attentive when dining out or being invited to someone's home. Wait for your host or hostess to show you where to sit and when to start eating. Follow their lead on whether to use utensils or your hands for certain dishes. Try everything that is offered to you and complements the food. Do not leave any food on your plate unless you are full. Offer to help with the dishes or clean up afterwards.

Tip generously for good service in restaurants, bars, taxis, or hotels. The usual amount is 10% of the bill, but you can tip more if you are very satisfied. Do not tip in coins or small bills, as this may be seen as insulting.

Festivals and traditions: Ibiza has a colourful culture that is expressed through various festivals and traditions throughout the year. These events celebrate the history, identity, and spirit of the island and its people. Some of the most important and popular festivals and traditions are:

Carnival: This is a festive period that takes place before Lent, usually in February or March. It involves parades, costumes, music, dancing, and parties in the streets. The carnival is a time to have fun and let go of inhibitions.

Easter: This is a religious celebration that commemorates the death and resurrection of Jesus Christ. It involves processions, masses, rituals, and decorations in the churches and towns. Easter is also a time to enjoy traditional food such as flaó (a cheesecake) or orelletes (a fried pastry).

Patron saint festivities: These are local celebrations that honour the patron saints of each town or village on the island. They involve religious ceremonies, folk dances, music, crafts, food, and fireworks. Some of the most famous patron saint festivities are Santa Eulària des Riu (February 12), Sant Antoni de Portmany (January 17), Sant Joan de Labritja (June 24), Sant Josep de Sa Talaia (March 19), Sant Francesc Xavier (December 3), Eivissa (August 8), Formentera (July 25).

We hope this information helps you understand some of the cultural norms and customs in Ibiza. We wish you a happy and enjoyable holiday!

Dining Etiquette

Ibiza is a gastronomic paradise, where you can enjoy a variety of cuisines, from traditional Mediterranean dishes to international fusion creations. However, there are also some dining etiquette rules that you should follow and respect when eating out on the island. Below are some of the main things you need to know:

Timing: The locals in Ibiza have a different meal schedule than most other countries. They usually have a light breakfast around 8 or 9 am, a late lunch around 2 or 3 pm, and a late dinner around 9 or 10 pm. This means that most restaurants open and close later than usual, and some may even close during the afternoon for a siesta. If you want to eat at the same time as the locals, you should adjust your clock accordingly. However, if you prefer to eat earlier or later, you can still find some places that cater to different timetables, especially in tourist areas.

Reservations: Ibiza is a popular destination, especially during the high season from June to September. This means that many restaurants can be very busy and crowded, especially during peak hours. Therefore, it is advisable to make reservations in advance, especially for popular or upscale places. You can call the restaurant directly or use online platforms such as The Fork or OpenTable to book your table. If you don't have a reservation, you may have to wait for a long time or be turned away.

Tipping: Tipping is not mandatory in Ibiza, but it is appreciated as a sign of gratitude for good service. The usual amount is 10% of the bill, but you can tip more if you are very satisfied. Do not tip in coins or small bills, as this may be seen as insulting. You can leave the tip on the table or hand it to the waiter when paying the bill.

Manners: The locals in Ibiza are generally relaxed and informal, but they also appreciate good manners and respect. Some basic manners and rules to follow are:

Greet the staff and other diners when entering or leaving the restaurant. A simple "hola" (hello) or "adiós" (goodbye) will do.

Wait for your host or hostess to show you where to sit and when to start eating. Follow their lead on whether to use utensils or your hands for certain dishes.

Use your napkin to wipe your mouth and hands, and place it on your lap when not using it. Do not use it to blow your nose or clean your glasses.

Chew with your mouth closed and do not talk with food in your mouth. Do not slurp, burp, or make loud noises when eating or drinking.

Do not put your elbows on the table or rest your feet on the chairs or benches. Do not play with your food or utensils.

Ask for permission before taking food from someone else's plate or serving yourself from a shared dish. Use the proper utensils or bread to do so.

Compliment the food and thank the chef and the staff for their service. Do not complain or criticize the food or service in front of them.

Do not ask for a doggy bag or take leftovers home, unless it is a casual place that offers this option.

Do not smoke inside the restaurant or near other diners who may be bothered by it. Ask for permission before lighting up outside or in designated areas.

We hope this information helps you learn some dining etiquette rules in Ibiza. We wish you a happy and delicious holiday!

Dress Code and Fashion in Ibiza

Ibiza is a fashionable and fun island, where you can express your style and personality through your outfits. However, there are also some dress codes and fashion tips that you should follow and respect when visiting the island. Below are some of the main things you need to know:

Climate: Ibiza has a Mediterranean climate, with hot and sunny summers and mild and rainy winters. The average temperature in summer is around 26°C, while in winter it is around 12°C. The island also has a sea breeze that can make it feel cooler or warmer depending on the direction. Therefore, you should pack clothes that are suitable for the season and the weather. In summer, opt for light and breathable fabrics, such as cotton, linen, or silk. In winter, layer up with warm and cosy fabrics, such as wool, fleece, or leather.

Occasion: You should pack clothes that are appropriate

for the occasion and the place. For the beach, wear swimsuits, cover-ups, sunglasses, hats, and sandals. For the clubs, wear dresses, skirts, tops, jeans, shorts, and shoes that are comfortable and stylish. For restaurants, wear smart casual or chic outfits that are elegant and sophisticated. For activities, wear sporty or casual outfits that are practical and functional.

Style: Ibiza has a relaxed and informal vibe, where you can wear whatever you like. However, there are also some style trends and influences that you can follow or incorporate into your outfits. Some of the most popular styles in Ibiza are:

Boho-chic: This style is inspired by the hippie culture and the natural beauty of the island. It features flowing dresses, skirts, tops, and pants in floral, ethnic, or tie-dye prints. It also features accessories such as hats, scarves, jewellery, bags, and shoes in leather, suede, or fringe.

Glam-rock: This style is inspired by the music and nightlife scene of the island. It features edgy dresses, skirts, tops, jeans, shorts, and jackets in black, silver, or metallic colours. It also features accessories such as sunglasses, belts, jewellery, bags, and shoes in studs, chains, or glitter.

Minimalist: This style is inspired by the modern and sophisticated vibe of the island. It features simple dresses, skirts, tops, jeans, shorts, and blazers in neutral, pastel, or monochrome colours. It also features accessories such as sunglasses, watches, jewellery, bags, and shoes in sleek, smooth, or geometric shapes.

We hope this information helps you plan your dress code and fashion in Ibiza. We wish you a happy and stylish holiday!

Festivals and Celebrations

Ibiza is a festive island, where you can enjoy a variety of festivals and celebrations throughout the year. Below are some of the main festivals and celebrations that you should not miss when visiting the island:

Epiphany: This is a religious festival that takes place on the 6th of January, marking the end of the Christmas season. It commemorates the visit of the three wise men to baby Jesus, bringing him gifts of gold, frankincense, and myrrh. On the eve of Epiphany, there are parades of floats with actors dressed as the three kings, who throw candies and presents to the children. The next day, there are masses and ceremonies in the churches, as well as traditional food such as roscón de Reyes (a ring-shaped cake with candied fruits) and chocolate con churros (hot chocolate with fried dough sticks).

Carnival: This is a festive period that takes place before Lent, usually in February or March. It involves parades, costumes, music, dancing, and parties in the streets. The carnival is a time to have fun and let go of inhibitions. Each town or village has its carnival theme and activities, but some of the most famous ones are in Ibiza Town, San Antonio, Santa Eulalia, and San Jose.

Easter: This is a religious celebration that commemorates the death and resurrection of Jesus Christ. It involves processions, masses, rituals, and decorations in the churches and towns. Easter is also a time to enjoy traditional food such as flaó (a cheesecake) or orelletes (a fried pastry).

Festa de Maig: This is a spring festival that takes place in May in Santa Eulalia, one of the oldest towns on the island. It celebrates the patron saint of the town, Santa Eulalia del Río, as well as the arrival of spring. It features floral decorations, folk dances, music, crafts, food, and fireworks.

Ibiza International Film Festival: This is a cultural event that takes place in May in Ibiza Town. It showcases a variety of films from different genres and countries, as well as workshops, panels, and awards. The festival aims to promote independent cinema and support local filmmakers.

Medieval Fair: This is a historical event that takes place in May in Ibiza Town. It celebrates the declaration of Ibiza Town as a World Heritage Site by UNESCO in 1999. It transforms the old town into a medieval market with stalls, crafts, food, and entertainment. There are also historical reenactments, shows, exhibitions, and concerts.

Ibiza Rocks: This is a musical event that takes place from June to September at the Ibiza Rocks Hotel in San Antonio. It features live performances from some of the biggest names in music, such as Arctic Monkeys, Bastille, and Stormzy. Ibiza Rocks also host pool parties, club nights, and boat parties throughout the summer season.

Patron Saint Festivities: These are local celebrations that honour the patron saints of each town or village on the island. They involve religious ceremonies, folk dances, music, crafts, food, and fireworks. Some of the most famous patron saint festivities are Santa Eulària des Riu (February 12), Sant Antoni de Portmany

(January 17), Sant Joan de Labritja (June 24), Sant Josep de Sa Talaia (March 19), Sant Francesc Xavier (December 3), Eivissa (August 8), Formentera (July 25).

International Music Summit: This is an electronic music conference and festival that takes place in May or June in Ibiza Town. The conference features industry panels, workshops, and networking events, while the festival includes performances from some of the top DJs and producers in the world.

Benimussa Park: This is a unique venue that hosts various events throughout the year, such as The Zoo Project, which is a themed party with costumes, music, art, and entertainment.

Closing Parties: These are the final parties that mark the end of the summer season in September or October. They take place at some of the most famous clubs on the island, such as Pacha, Amnesia, Ushuaia, Hï Ibiza, Privilege, or DC10.

Dia del Carmen: This is a religious festival that takes place on the 16th of July. It celebrates the patron saint of fishermen and sailors, the Virgin of Carmen. It involves processions of boats decorated with flowers and flags, as well as masses and blessings at the ports and beaches.

Halloween: This is a popular celebration that takes

place on the 31st of October. It involves dressing up in costumes, carving pumpkins, trick-or-treating, and attending parties at various venues on the island.

We hope this information helps you plan your festivals and celebrations in Ibiza. We wish you a happy and festive holiday!

Chapter 4 • Exploring Ibiza's Regions

Ibiza Town and South Coast

Ibiza Town, or Eivissa in Catalan, is the capital and the largest city of Ibiza, a Spanish island in the Mediterranean Sea. It is one of the oldest towns in Europe, dating back to the 7th century BC when it was founded by the Carthaginians. Today, it is a UNESCO World Heritage Site, with a rich cultural heritage and a vibrant nightlife.

Ibiza Town is divided into two main parts: the old town (Dalt Vila) and the new town (Eixample). The old town is surrounded by colossal medieval walls that offer stunning views of the city and the sea. Inside the walls, you can explore the maze of cobbled streets, where you will find historical monuments, museums, art galleries, shops, and restaurants. The most notable landmarks are the Gothic cathedral, the Catalan castle, and the Portal de ses Taules, the main archway entrance to the old town.

The new town is where most of the modern amenities and attractions are located. It has a lively marina, where you can see luxury yachts and sailboats, as well as a promenade with cafes, bars, and clubs. The new town is also home to some of the most famous clubs in the world, such as Pacha, Lio, and Heart. These clubs attract thousands of visitors every year, who come to enjoy the music of the world's top DJs and celebrities.

The south coast of Ibiza is known for its beautiful beaches and coves, where you can relax, swim, sunbathe, or practice water sports. Some of the most popular beaches are Ses Salines, Es Cavallet, Playa d'en Bossa, Cala Jondal, and Sa Caleta. These beaches have crystal-clear water, fine sand, and natural scenery. They also have a variety of facilities and services, such as restaurants, bars, sunbeds, umbrellas, showers, and lifeguards.

The south coast of Ibiza also has some hidden gems that are worth discovering. For example, you can visit Es Vedra, a mysterious rock island that rises from the sea and is said to have magical powers. You can also explore Atlantis, a secret cove that was carved by hippies in the 1960s and has stunning rock formations and pools. Or you can admire Es Cubells, a charming village that overlooks the sea and has a white-washed church and a peaceful atmosphere.

Ibiza Town and South Coast are two of the most attractive and exciting areas of Ibiza. They offer a perfect combination of history, culture, nature, and entertainment.

Dalt Vila: the old town

Dalt Vila, which means "High Town" in Catalan, is the historical and cultural heart of Ibiza. It is a UNESCO World Heritage Site that preserves the legacy of more than 2,500 years of history, from the Phoenicians to the present day. Dalt Vila is a place where you can admire the architecture, art, and traditions of Ibiza, as well as enjoy the views, the atmosphere, and the nightlife.

Dalt Vila is located on a hill overlooking the sea and the modern city of Ibiza. It is surrounded by impressive Renaissance walls that were built in the 16th century by the Spanish kings to protect the island from invasions. The walls have seven bastions, each with a different name and function. You can walk along the walls and enjoy panoramic views of the city, the port, and the countryside.

There are two main entrances to Dalt Vila: Portal de ses Taules and Portal Nou. Portal de ses Taules is the most dramatic one, with a stone drawbridge and two Roman statues guarding the gate. Once you enter, you will find yourself in a cobbled courtyard with a coat of arms and a plaque that declares Dalt Vila as a World Heritage Site. From there, you can access Plaza de Vila, the main square of the old town, where you will find cosy restaurants, art galleries, and craft shops.

Portal Nou is a more gradual entrance, with a ramp that leads to a small chapel and a garden. This entrance is closer to Museo Puig des Molins, an archaeological museum that houses an impressive collection of artefacts from the Carthaginian era, including burial grounds and Roman remains.

Inside Dalt Vila, you can explore the narrow and winding streets that reveal the history of the old town. You will see whitewashed houses with colourful flowers, ancient churches and convents, medieval towers and palaces, and hidden corners that invite you to discover their secrets. Some of the highlights are:

The Cathedral of Santa Maria: A Gothic church that was built on the site of a former mosque. It has a beautiful cloister and a museum with religious art.

The Castle: A medieval fortress that dominates the summit of Dalt Vila. It has several rooms and courtyards that host cultural events and exhibitions.

The Portal de ses Taules: The main archway entrance to Dalt Vila has a spectacular patio of arms and a wooden drawbridge.

The Contemporary Art Museum: A modern museum that showcases works by local and international artists. It also has an underground section where you can see an ancient Phoenician house.

The Almudaina: A palace that was once the residence of the Muslim governors of Ibiza. It has a Moorish style and a beautiful garden.

Dalt Vila is not only a place to visit during the day but also at night. It has a lively nightlife scene, with some of the most famous clubs in Ibiza. These clubs offer music, entertainment, and glamour for all tastes and budgets. You can also enjoy a romantic dinner or a drink in one of the many bars and restaurants that offer stunning views of the illuminated city.

Dalt Vila is a must-see destination for anyone who wants to experience the essence of Ibiza. It is a place where history, culture, nature, and fun coexist in harmony.

La Marina: the harbour district

La Marina, or The Harbour District, is the area that stretches along the seafront of Ibiza Town, from the old port to the new marina. It is one of the most lively and cosmopolitan parts of the city, where you can enjoy the maritime atmosphere, the cultural diversity, and the entertainment options.

La Marina has a long history as a fishing and trading port, dating back to the Phoenician times. It was also a strategic point for the defence of the island, as it witnessed many battles and invasions. Today, it is a modern and dynamic port, where you can see all kinds of boats, from traditional fishing vessels to luxury yachts.

La Marina is divided into two sections: the old port and the new marina. The old port is where you can find the ferry terminal, where you can catch a boat to

Formentera or other destinations. It is also where you can visit the fish market, where you can buy fresh seafood or watch the fishermen unload their catch. The old port has a charming and authentic vibe, with narrow streets, old buildings, and local shops.

The new marina is where you can find Marina Ibiza, a yachting and lifestyle destination like no other in the world. It is an exclusive and sophisticated place, where you can moor your boat, enjoy the services and facilities, or simply admire the views. The new marina has a glamorous and cosmopolitan vibe, with high-end shops, restaurants, bars, and clubs.

Talamanca: the nearest beach

If you are looking for a beach that is close to Ibiza Town, but still offers a peaceful and relaxing atmosphere, Talamanca might be the perfect choice for you. Talamanca is the longest beach in Ibiza Town, with a length of about 900 meters and a width of 25 meters. It is located on the north side of Ibiza Town, just 15 minutes walk along the marina from the city center.

Talamanca is a sandy beach with shallow and clear

water, ideal for swimming, sunbathing, or practising water sports. The water is usually calm, as the beach is protected by a bay and a small island called Illa de Talamanca. The beach has a natural and authentic vibe, with some areas covered by seaweed and stones, which provide a habitat for marine life. You can also enjoy the views of Dalt Vila, the old town of Ibiza, and the hills of Cap Martinet from the beach.

Talamanca has a variety of facilities and services to make your stay comfortable and enjoyable. You can find sunbeds, umbrellas, showers, lifeguards, and access for people with reduced mobility on the beach. You can also rent kayaks, paddle boards, or pedal boats to explore the coast. If you are hungry or thirsty, you can choose from a wide range of bars and restaurants that line the beachfront, offering local and international cuisine. Some of the most popular places are The Fish Shack, Sa Punta de Talamanca, and Chambao Family Beach Club.

Playa d'en Bossa: the party hotspot

If you are looking for a beach that is close to Ibiza Town, and also offers a non-stop party atmosphere, Playa d'en Bossa might be the perfect choice for you. Playa d'en

Bossa is the longest beach in Ibiza Island, with a length of about 2.5 km and a width of 30 meters. It is located on the south side of Ibiza Town, just a 10-minute drive from the airport.

Playa d'en Bossa is a sandy beach with clear and warm water, ideal for swimming, sunbathing, or practising water sports. The water is usually calm, as the beach is protected by a bay and a small island called Illa de ses Rates. The beach has a modern and trendy vibe, with stylish sunbeds and umbrellas.

Playa d'en Bossa has a nice nightlife scene, with some of the best clubs in Ibiza, such as Ushuaia, Space, and Bora Bora. It does not matter if you are looking for a relaxing stroll or an exciting adventure, you will find something to suit your preferences in Playa d'en Bossa.

Ses Salines: the nature reserve and beach

Ses Salines is a nature reserve and a beach that are located in the south of Ibiza, near the airport. They are part of the Ses Salines Natural Park, which covers both the salt flats of Ibiza and Formentera, as well as the sea channel between them. Ses Salines is a UNESCO World Heritage Site, as it is home to a rich biodiversity and a cultural heritage that dates back to the Phoenician times.

Ses Salines Nature Reserve is a protected area that spans over 3,000 hectares of land and 13,000 hectares of sea. It is one of the most important wetlands in the Mediterranean, as it hosts a variety of habitats, such as salt marshes, sand dunes, pine forests, and rocky shores.

It is also a refuge for many species of plants and animals, especially birds, such as flamingos, herons, egrets, and ospreys. You can visit the nature reserve by car, bike, or foot, and enjoy the scenery and the wildlife. You can also learn more about the conservation efforts and the salt production at the visitor center in San Jose.

Ses Salines Beach is a trendy and popular beach that attracts visitors from all over the world. It is about 1.5 km long and 25 to 30 meters wide, with fine white sand and clear turquoise water. It is surrounded by dense forests of junipers and pine trees, which provide shade and privacy. It is also close to the old salt pans, which add a touch of charm and history to the landscape. The beach has a range of facilities and services, such as sunbeds, umbrellas, showers, lifeguards, and access for people with reduced mobility.

If you are hungry or thirsty, you can choose from a wide range of bars and restaurants that line the beachfront, offering local and international cuisine. Some of the most famous places are Sa Trinxa, Malibu Beach Club, and Jockey Club. You can also enjoy music and entertainment at venues such as Ushuaia Beach Hotel, Hard Rock Hotel, or Nassau Beach Club.

Sa Caleta: the Phoenician site and cove

Sa Caleta, or Es Bol Nou, is a small and secluded cove located in the south of Ibiza, near the airport. It is one of the most unique and charming places on the island, as it combines natural beauty, historical significance, and cultural diversity.

Sa Caleta is best known for being the site of the first Phoenician settlement in Ibiza, dating back to the 8th century BC. The Phoenicians were a seafaring people who came from the eastern Mediterranean and established trade routes and colonies throughout the region. They chose Sa Caleta as their base because of its strategic location, its sheltered bay, and its abundant resources. They built a fortified town with houses, workshops, temples, and a necropolis, where they lived for about two centuries before moving to a larger site in Ibiza Town.

The Phoenician site of Sa Caleta was declared a UNESCO World Heritage Site in 1999, as it is one of the best preserved examples of Phoenician urbanism in the Mediterranean. You can visit the site by following a wooden walkway that leads you through the ruins and offers informative panels and stunning views of the sea and the cliffs. You can also learn more about the history and culture of the Phoenicians at the Archaeological Museum of Ibiza, where you can see artifacts and exhibits from the site.

Sa Caleta is also a beautiful cove that offers a relaxing and authentic beach experience. It is about 100 meters long and 10 meters wide, with fine golden sand and clear blue water. It is surrounded by reddish cliffs that are covered by pine trees and junipers, which create a striking contrast with the sea and the sky. The cove has a natural and rustic vibe, with some areas of rocks and seaweed that provide habitat for marine life. You can swim, snorkel, or sunbathe on the beach, or enjoy the shade and privacy under the trees.

If you are hungry or thirsty, you can choose from a wide range of bars and restaurants that line the beachfront, offering local and international cuisine. One of the most famous places is Restaurante Sa Caleta, where you can taste delicious seafood dishes, such as bullit de peix (fish stew), paella, or caldereta de langosta (lobster stew).

Es Cavallet: the nudist beach

Es Cavallet is a nudist beach located in the south of Ibiza, near the airport. It is part of the Ses Salines Natural Park, a UNESCO World Heritage Site that covers both the salt flats of Ibiza and Formentera, as well as the sea channel between them. Es Cavallet is one of the most beautiful and natural beaches on the island, with fine white sand, clear turquoise water, and stunning views of Dalt Vila, the old town of Ibiza.

Es Cavallet is about 1.5 km long and 25 to 30 meters wide, with some areas of rocks and seaweed that provide habitat for marine life. The beach has a relaxed and friendly vibe, with people of all ages, genders, and orientations enjoying the sun and the sea in their birthday suits. Nudism is not mandatory, but it is highly recommended, as it is part of the culture and tradition of Es Cavallet.

If you are hungry or thirsty, you can choose from a wide range of bars and restaurants that line the beachfront, offering local and international cuisine. Some of the most famous places are El Chiringuito, where you can taste delicious seafood dishes, such as bullit de peix (fish stew), paella, or caldereta de langosta (lobster stew), Sa Trinxa, where you can enjoy music, entertainment, and cocktails in a bohemian atmosphere, and Chiringay, where you can join the vibrant gay scene and party until sunset.

It has a lively nightlife scene, with some of the best parties in Ibiza. You can enjoy music and glamour at venues such as Ushuaia Beach Hotel, Hard Rock Hotel, or Nassau Beach Club. You can also enjoy a romantic dinner or a drink in one of the many bars and restaurants.

Recommendations for Accommodation

If you are looking for accommodation in Ibiza Town and South Coast, you have a wide range of options to choose from. You can find hotels, apartments, villas, hostels, and campsites that cater to different needs and preferences. Below are some of the best accommodation in Ibiza Town and South Coast that we recommend:

Rooftop Experimental Montesol: This is a 5-star hotel located in the heart of Ibiza Town, near the port and the old town. It has 33 rooms and suites with balconies, air conditioning, satellite TV, minibar, and private bathroom. It also has a rooftop terrace with a bar and sea views, a restaurant with Mediterranean cuisine, a spa with crystal walls, and a 24-hour reception. Rooftop Experimental Montesol is a luxury hotel that offers excellent service and facilities.

Sir Joan Hotel: This is a 4-star hotel located on the seafront near Ibiza Town, close to Marina Botafoch Harbour. It has 38 rooms and suites with balconies, air conditioning, satellite TV, minibar, safe, free WiFi, and private bathroom. It also has an outdoor pool with sun loungers, a restaurant with Asian fusion cuisine, a bar with cocktails and music, and a 24-hour reception. Sir Joan Hotel is a stylish and elegant hotel that offers high-quality service and facilities.

Sud Ibiza Suites: This is an apartment complex located on the beachfront near Ibiza Town, close to Figueretas Beach. It has 34 apartments with balconies, air conditioning, satellite TV, kitchenette, coffee machine, free WiFi, and private bathroom. It also has a terrace with seasonal solarium and jacuzzi, views of the sea, and a 24-hour reception. Sud Ibiza Suites is a modern and comfortable apartment complex that offers spacious and well-equipped apartments.

Finca Can Toni: This is a country house located in the countryside near Ibiza Town, surrounded by gardens and olive trees. It has 10 rooms with air conditioning, satellite TV, free WiFi, safe, and private bathroom. It also has an outdoor pool with sun loungers, a restaurant with local cuisine, a massage area, and free parking. Finca Can Toni is a charming country house that offers relaxing and authentic accommodation.

These are some of the best accommodation in Ibiza Town and South Coast that we recommend. We hope you enjoy your stay in Ibiza Town and South Coast.

Recommendations for Restaurants

If you are looking for restaurants in Ibiza Town and South Coast, you have a wide range of options to choose from. You can find restaurants that offer local and international cuisine, with fresh seafood, grilled meat, salads, paellas, pizzas, sushi, and more. You can also find restaurants that offer different settings and atmospheres, such as beachfront, countryside, terrace, or rooftop. Below are some of the best restaurants in Ibiza Town and South Coast that we recommend:

Cala Bonita: This is a restaurant located on the beachfront of S'Estanyol, one of the most beautiful and natural beaches on the island. It offers high-quality Mediterranean cuisine with a local touch in a peaceful setting beside the sea. You can enjoy dishes such as gazpacho, seafood rice, grilled fish, or almond cake. You can also enjoy views of the sea and the nearby islands from the terrace.

Experimental Beach: This is a restaurant located on the beachfront of Ses Salines Natural Park, near the airport. It offers French cuisine with a fusion touch in a lively setting with music and cocktails. You can enjoy dishes such as tuna tartare, octopus salad, lamb chops, or cheesecake. You can also enjoy views of the sea and the sunset from the terrace.

La Gaia by Oscar Molina: This is a restaurant located in the 5-star hotel Grand Palladium Palace Ibiza Resort & Spa, near Playa d'en Bossa. It offers Japanese-Peruvian cuisine with innovative and exquisite dishes in an elegant setting with art and design. You can enjoy dishes such as scallop carpaccio, duck breast, or chocolate soufflé. You can also enjoy views of the pool and the garden from the terrace.

Es Ventall: This is a restaurant located in the center of San Antonio, near the port. It offers Mediterranean cuisine with local products in a charming setting with white walls and wooden furniture. You can enjoy dishes such as gazpacho, seafood rice, grilled fish, or almond cake. You can also enjoy views of the town and the church from the terrace.

Los Enamorados: This is a restaurant located on the seafront near Portinatx, where you can enjoy stunning views of the sea and the cliffs. It has a Cuban-inspired design and atmosphere, with wooden tables and chairs, cushions, and neon lights. It offers Japanese and Peruvian fusion cuisine with fresh Ibizan seafood, such as scallop carpaccio, ceviche, sushi, or miso cod. It also has a bar with cocktails and music, and a boutique with clothing and accessories. Los Enamorados is a stylish and lively restaurant that offers high-quality service and facilities.

These are some of the best restaurants in Ibiza Town and South Coast that we recommend. You can find more information about them on their websites. We hope you enjoy your meal in Ibiza Town and South Coast.

San Antonio and West Coast

San Antonio, or Sant Antoni de Portmany in Catalan, is the second largest town and municipality in Ibiza, an island in the Mediterranean Sea that is famous for its nightlife and beaches. San Antonio is located on the western coast of Ibiza, about 18 km from Ibiza Town, the capital and the largest city of the island. San Antonio has a long history as a fishing and trading port, dating back to the Phoenician times. It was also a strategic point for the defense of the island, as it witnessed many battles and invasions.

Today, San Antonio is one of the most popular and lively resorts in Ibiza, attracting visitors from all over the world, especially young Brits who come to enjoy the music, the entertainment, and the party scene. San Antonio has some of the best clubs in Ibiza, such as Eden, Es Paradis, and Ibiza Rocks Hotel.

San Antonio also has a vibrant bar scene, especially in the infamous 'west end', a strip of bars and clubs that offer various drink deals and music genres. One of the most iconic places in San Antonio is the Sunset Strip, a promenade along the seafront where you can watch the stunning sunset while listening to chill-out music at venues such as Café del Mar, Café Mambo, or Savannah.

San Antonio is not only about nightlife, but also about nature and culture. San Antonio has a beautiful bay that offers a variety of water sports and activities, such as kayaking, paddle boarding, jet skiing, or glass-bottom boat trips. You can also visit some of the nearby beaches and coves that offer a more relaxing and authentic atmosphere, such as Cala Salada, Cala Gracio, or Cala Bassa. If you are interested in history and art, you can visit the Church of San Antonio, which dates back to the 14th century and has a fascinating collection of paintings and sculptures. You can also visit the Egg of Columbus, a monument that commemorates the discovery of

America by Christopher Columbus, who is said to have been born in Ibiza.

The west coast of Ibiza is not only San Antonio, but also other charming towns and villages that offer a different perspective of the island. The west coast of Ibiza has some of the most beautiful and natural beaches and coves on the island, such as Cala Conta, Cala Tarida, or Cala d'Hort. These beaches have crystal-clear water, fine sand, and natural scenery. They also have a variety of facilities and services.

San Antonio: the sunset strip and nightlife

San Antonio, or Sant Antoni de Portmany in Catalan, is the second largest town in Ibiza. The Sunset Strip needs little introduction - you might not know all of it, so here's our guide on where to go and what to do when you get there.

The Sunset Strip is a long strip replete with vibrant bars where the sun sinks into the sea in a spectacle of glorious colour, to an eclectic soundtrack that captures the essence of the Balearic Beat. A trip to San Antonio's

Sunset Strip should definitely be on your list when visiting Ibiza. Known locally as "Ses Variades", this long and popular promenade extends all the way from the harbour to the small beach of Caló des Moro and a bit beyond. It is probably the island's most visited location and with good reason. Sunsets here are very special for a couple of reasons. Being a small island, Ibiza has nice clean air and the wide open sea next to the Strip means colours refract more easily. This results in a light show that everyone agrees is nothing short of spectacular, with a colour palate that expands from orange and yellow to pink, violet and hues of red.

The whole area is alive with people, extravagant club parades, street artists, including those doing fire shows, and people just sitting on the rocks - all adoring the sun. All bars and restaurants serve a variety of dishes with cuisine influences from around the world as well as full-on dining experiences, where you can splash out and treat yourself. There are also affordable pizzas, homemade burgers, smaller plates and snacks on offer. When dining, it's essential to book a table beforehand.

Music makes the ideal partner for the setting sun, with many of the venues offering a variation of those Balearic chill-out sounds for which the Strip has become famous. It all started back in 1980, when Café del Mar, with the help from DJ José Padilla, added a soundtrack to the sunset and changed this once sleepy promenade forever.

It was this venue that really created the chill-out genre and many compilation albums, for which it has gained worldwide fame. Café Mambo and Savannah, now also well known over a number of years for their popular music compilations, came next and after that more and more sunset venues lined the promenade. When space on the original Sunset Strip ran out, new sunset bars started to open, expanding the original promenade all the way.

Cala Salada: the scenic beach

Cala Salada is a scenic beach located in the west coast of Ibiza, near San Antonio. It is one of the most beautiful and natural beaches on the island, with fine golden sand, clear blue water, and stunning views of the sea and the cliffs. It is surrounded by reddish cliffs that are covered by pine trees and junipers, which create a striking contrast with the sea and the sky. The beach has a relaxed and friendly vibe, with people of all ages, genders, and orientations enjoying the sun and the sea.

Cala Salada is about 200 meters long and 30 meters wide, with some areas of rocks and seaweed that provide habitat for marine life. It is ideal for swimming, snorkeling, or sunbathing on the beach, or enjoying the shade and privacy under the trees. The water is usually calm, as the beach is protected by a bay and a small island called Sa Conillera.

One of the most famous places is Restaurante Cala Salada, where you can taste delicious seafood dishes, such as bullit de peix (fish stew), paella, or caldereta de langosta (lobster stew).

Cala Salada is also close to another smaller and more secluded cove called Cala Saladeta, which is separated from Cala Salada by some rocky cliffs with a group of old fishermen cabins. Cala Saladeta has a similar landscape and atmosphere to Cala Salada, but it is more peaceful and less crowded. You can access Cala Saladeta by walking along a path that goes around the cliffs or by swimming across the bay. Cala Saladeta is a perfect place to escape from the hustle and bustle of Cala Salada and enjoy a more relaxing and authentic experience.

Cala Bassa: the chic beach club

Cala Bassa is not only a scenic beach, but also a chic beach club that offers a luxurious and exclusive experience. Cala Bassa Beach Club, or CBBC for short, is a stylish and elegant venue that combines the natural beauty of the beach with the comfort and convenience of the club. CBBC has four restaurants, two bars, a boutique, a massage area, and a VIP zone, where you can enjoy the best service and facilities on the island.

CBBC has four restaurants that cater to different tastes and occasions. You can choose from:

CBBC Restaurant: A Mediterranean restaurant that serves fresh seafood, grilled meat, salads, and paellas. It has a spacious terrace with stunning views of the sea and the cliffs.

CBBC Sushi: A Japanese restaurant that offers high-quality sushi, sashimi, nigiri, and other delicacies. It has a cozy and intimate atmosphere with wooden tables and cushions.

CBBC Snack: A casual restaurant that offers burgers, sandwiches, pizzas, salads, and snacks. It has a relaxed and friendly vibe with colorful chairs and umbrellas.

CBBC Chiringo: A traditional beach bar that offers

tapas, sandwiches, drinks, and ice creams. It has a rustic and authentic vibe with wooden tables and benches.

CBBC has two bars that offer a variety of drinks and cocktails. You can choose from:

CBBC Cocktail Bar: A sophisticated bar that offers classic and signature cocktails, such as mojitos, daiquiris, margaritas, and caipirinhas. It has a modern and elegant design with white sofas and tables.

CBBC Music Bar: A lively bar that offers music, entertainment, and fun. It has DJs, live bands, shows, and events throughout the day and night. It has a colorful design with neon lights and speakers.

CBBC also has other facilities and services to make your stay comfortable and enjoyable. You can find:

CBBC Boutique: A shop that sells clothing, accessories, souvenirs, and gifts. It has a chic and trendy design with white shelves and racks.

CBBC Massage: A massage area that offers relaxing and therapeutic massages. It has a peaceful and serene design with white curtains and beds.

CBBC VIP: A VIP zone that offers privacy and exclusivity. It has sunbeds, umbrellas, showers, lockers, towels, magazines, drinks, snacks, and personal assistants.

Cala Conta: the stunning views and turquoise waters

Cala Conta, or Platges de Comte in Catalan, is one of the most beautiful and natural beaches on the island of Ibiza, located on the west coast, near San Antonio. Cala Conta offers stunning views of the little islands dotted near Ibiza's coastline, such as Illa des Bosc, Illa des Conillera, and S'Espartar. The water is clear and turquoise, with shades of blue and green that change depending on the sunlight and the depth. The sand is fine and white, with some areas of rocks and seaweed that provide habitat for marine life.

Cala Conta is composed of two main beaches and a smaller cove that are separated by rocky outcrops. The first beach, which is closer to the parking area, is about 800 meters long and 15 to 30 meters wide. The second beach, which is further away from the parking area, is about 200 meters long and 10 to 15 meters wide. It has fewer facilities and services, but it is more peaceful and less crowded. It also has a small chiringuito (beach bar) that serves drinks and snacks. The smaller cove, which is called Cala Escondida (the hidden cove), is at the far west end and can be reached by walking along a path that goes around the cliffs or by swimming across the bay. It is popular with nudists and has a natural and rustic vibe.

Cala Conta is ideal for swimming, snorkeling, or sunbathing on the beach, or enjoying the shade and privacy under the trees. The water is usually calm, as the beach is protected by a bay and a small island called Sa Conillera. However, be careful when swimming into the open sea; there are very strong currents here - so even more experienced swimmers should avoid aiming for the island offshore. The many rocky outcrops also make Cala Conta an interesting place for snorkeling, as you can see a variety of fish and other marine creatures.

Cala Tarida: the family-friendly resort

Cala Tarida is a family-friendly resort located on the west coast of Ibiza, near San Antonio. It is one of the most complete and natural beaches on the island, with fine golden sand, clear turquoise water, and stunning views of the sea and the cliffs. Cala Tarida is about 800 meters long and 15 to 30 meters wide, with some areas of rocks and seaweed.

One of the most famous places is Restaurante Cala Tarida, where you can taste delicious seafood dishes, such as bullit de peix (fish stew), paella, or caldereta de langosta (lobster stew).

Cala Tarida is also close to other charming towns and villages that offer a different perspective of the island. You can visit San José, a picturesque village that has a white-washed church and a peaceful atmosphere. You can also visit San Antonio, a lively town that has a beautiful bay, a promenade, and a sunset strip. Or you can visit Cala Conta, another scenic beach that has clear and turquoise water, fine sand, and stunning views of the little islands dotted near Ibiza's coastline.

Es Vedrà: the mysterious island

Es Vedrà is a small rocky island off the south-west coast of Ibiza. It is one of the most dramatic and iconic sights of Ibiza, as it rises majestically from the sea to a height of 413 meters. It is part of the Cala d'Hort nature reserve, which protects the biodiversity and the cultural heritage of the area. Es Vedrà is uninhabited, except for a colony of endangered Eleonora's falcons and a sub-species of the Ibizan wall lizard.

Es Vedrà is not only a natural wonder, but also a source of many myths and legends, that add to its mystery and allure. Some of the most popular stories are:

Es Vedrà is the third most magnetic spot on earth, after the North Pole and the Bermuda Triangle. This causes compasses to malfunction and strange phenomena to occur near the island. However, this is just a myth, as there is no scientific evidence to support it.

Es Vedrà is the tip of the sunken city of Atlantis, which was destroyed by a cataclysmic event in ancient times. Some people claim to have seen ruins and carvings under the water near the island. However, this is also a myth, as there is no archaeological proof to confirm it.

Es Vedrà is home to sirens and sea-nymphs, who tried to lure Odysseus from his ship in Homer's Odyssey. It is also thought to be the holy island of Tanit, the Phoenician lunar goddess, who was worshiped as the patroness of Ibiza. Some people believe that sacrifices were made to Tanit during full moons on the shore of the island.

Es Vedrà has magical and healing powers, that can enhance one's spiritual and physical well-being. It is also a place of meditation and enlightenment, where one can connect with higher realms and dimensions. Some people claim to have seen UFOs and orbs of light near the island.

Es Vedrà can be visited by different means, depending on your preferences and budget. You can:

Take a boat trip from San Antonio or Cala d'Hort, which will take you around or close to the island. You can enjoy the views, the wildlife, and the history of Es Vedrà from the sea.

Rent a kayak or a paddle board from Cala d'Hort or Cala Codolar, which will allow you to explore the coast and reach the island by yourself. You can swim, snorkel, or sunbathe on the rocks near Es Vedrà.

Hike from Cala d'Hort to Torre des Savinar, an old watchtower that offers panoramic views of Es Vedrà and the surrounding area. You can admire the scenery, take photos, or watch the sunset from this vantage point.

Recommendations for Accommodation

Below are some of the best accommodation in San Antonio and West Coast that we recommend:

Oda | Ibiza, Spain: This is a website that allows you to search and book properties for your stay in Ibiza. You can filter by location, price, rating, facilities, and more. You can also read reviews from other travelers and see photos of the properties. Oda offers some of the best deals and discounts for accommodation in San Antonio and West Coast.

Pikes Ibiza: This is a 5-star hotel located in the hills above San Antonio, where couples can enjoy a romantic and hedonistic experience. Pikes has 25 rooms and suites with balconies, air conditioning, satellite TV, minibar, and private bathroom. It also has an outdoor pool with sun loungers, a restaurant with Mediterranean cuisine, a bar with cocktails and music, and a spa with crystal walls. Pikes is a luxury hotel that offers excellent service and facilities.

Hostal La Torre: This is a 3-star hotel located on the seafront near San Antonio, where you can watch the stunning sunset while listening to chill-out music. La

Torre has 17 rooms with balconies, air conditioning, satellite TV, free WiFi, safe, and private bathroom. It also has a terrace with seasonal solarium and jacuzzi, views of the sea, and a restaurant with local cuisine. La Torre is a stylish and elegant hotel that offers high-quality service and facilities.

Las Mimosas: This is a 4-star hotel located on the quieter end of San Antonio Bay with spacious rooms and a pool you'll want to hang out around all day. Las Mimosas has 17 rooms with balconies, air conditioning, satellite TV, minibar, safe, free WiFi, and private bathroom. It also has an outdoor pool with sun loungers, a restaurant with Italian comfort food, a bar with cocktails and music, and a massage area. Las Mimosas is a modern and comfortable hotel that offers spacious and well-equipped rooms.

Cubanito Ibiza: This is a 4-star hotel located on the west coast of Ibiza with Cuban-inspired design and atmosphere. Cubanito has 32 rooms with balconies, air conditioning, satellite TV, minibar, safe, free WiFi, and private bathroom. It also has a rooftop terrace with a bar and sea views, a restaurant with Cuban fusion cuisine, a pool with sun loungers, and a 24-hour reception. Cubanito is a stylish and lively hotel that offers high-quality service and facilities.

Recommendations for Restaurants

If you are looking for restaurants in San Antonio and West Coast, you have a wide range of options to choose from. You can find restaurants that offer local and international cuisine, with fresh seafood, grilled meat, salads, paellas, pizzas, sushi, and more. You can also find restaurants that offer different settings and atmospheres, such as beachfront, countryside, terrace, or rooftop. Below are some of the best restaurants in San Antonio and West Coast that we recommend:

Tapas Ibiza: This is a restaurant located on the outskirts of San Antonio, near Cala Gració. It offers Mediterranean cuisine with a variety of tapas, such as patatas bravas, croquetas, tortilla española, or gambas al ajillo. It also has a terrace with views of the sea and the sunset. Tapas Ibiza is a restaurant that offers excellent service and quality.

Es Tragon: This is a restaurant located on the cliffs near Cala Gració. It is the first and only restaurant in Ibiza that has a Michelin star, which it received in 2019. It offers a seasonal menu with innovative and exquisite dishes, such as scallop carpaccio, duck breast, or chocolate soufflé. It also has a wine cellar with more than 200 references. Es Tragon is a restaurant that offers a luxurious and exclusive experience.

Es Ventall: This is a restaurant located in the center of San Antonio, near the port. It offers Mediterranean cuisine with local products, such as gazpacho, seafood rice, grilled fish, or almond cake. It also has a terrace with views of the town and the church. Es Ventall is a restaurant that offers charming and romantic experience.

Sa Capella: This is a restaurant located in the hills above San Antonio, in an old chapel that dates back to the 18th century. It has been serving fresh seafood since 1971, such as paella, fideuá, local prawns, lobster, and the famous Raó of Formentera. It also has a spacious terrace with stunning views of the sea and the cliffs. Sa Capella is a restaurant that offers excellent service and quality.

Los Enamorados: This is a restaurant located on the seafront near Portinatx, where you can enjoy stunning views of the sea and the cliffs. It has a Cuban-inspired design and atmosphere, with wooden tables and chairs, cushions, and neon lights. It offers Japanese and Peruvian fusion cuisine with fresh Ibizan seafood, such as scallop carpaccio, ceviche, sushi, or miso cod. It also has a bar with cocktails and music, and a boutique with clothing and accessories. Los Enamorados is a stylish and lively restaurant that offers high-quality service and facilities.

Santa Eulàlia and East Coast

If you are looking for a quieter and more laid-back destination in Ibiza, you might want to consider Santa Eulalia and the East Coast. This area offers a beautiful contrast between the green countryside and the blue sea, with plenty of charming villages, beaches, markets and restaurants to explore.

Santa Eulalia is the third largest town in Ibiza and the main hub of the East Coast. It has a lovely promenade along the white sandy beach, where you can enjoy a stroll or a bike ride, and a marina with some upscale boutiques and cafés. The town is well known for its gastronomy, especially seafood, and has a variety of dining options to suit every taste and budget.

The old town of Santa Eulalia is a must-see for its historical and cultural attractions. You can visit the church of Es Puig de Missa, which dates back to the 16th century and offers panoramic views of the town and the sea. You can also explore the Ethnographic Museum, which showcases the rural life and traditions of Ibiza in a typical farmhouse.

The East Coast has some of the best beaches in Ibiza, ranging from family-friendly coves to secluded bays. Some of the most popular ones are Es Niu Blau, Cala Llonga, Cala Nova and Cala Llenya. You can relax on the soft sand, swim in the clear water, or try some water sports such as kayaking, paddle boarding or sailing.

If you are in the mood for some shopping, you will not be disappointed by the markets on the East Coast. You can find local products, handicrafts, clothes, jewellery and more at the artisan market in Santa Eulalia, the hippy market of Punta Arabi in Es Canar, or the evening market in Cala Llonga. These markets are also great places to experience the bohemian vibe and the live music of Ibiza.

The East Coast is not known for its nightlife, but it does have some bars and pubs where you can have a drink and listen to some music. You can also catch some cultural events such as concerts, festivals or exhibitions in Santa Eulalia or nearby towns. If you want to experience the famous club scene of Ibiza, you can easily reach Ibiza Town or San Antonio by car or bus.

Santa Eulalia and the East Coast are ideal destinations for those who want to enjoy a relaxing holiday with a touch of culture in Ibiza. You can find accommodation options for every budget and preference, from luxury hotels to cozy villas. You can also rent a car or a bike to explore the area at your own pace.

Santa Eulàlia: the relaxed town and promenade

If you are looking for a peaceful and elegant destination in Ibiza, you might want to visit Santa Eulàlia, the third largest town on the island and the main centre of the East Coast. Santa Eulàlia has a lot to offer to its visitors, from its beautiful beach and promenade to its rich cultural and gastronomic heritage.

Santa Eulàlia's beach is one of the most attractive in Ibiza, with fine white sand and clear blue water. It is ideal for families, couples and anyone who wants to enjoy a relaxing day by the sea. The beach has all the facilities and services you need, such as sunbeds, umbrellas, showers, lifeguards, water sports and boat rentals.

The promenade along the beach is one of the highlights of Santa Eulàlia. It is a pleasant and lively place where you can walk, cycle or skate, admiring the views of the sea and the marina. The promenade is lined with palm trees, flowers and benches, as well as many cafés, restaurants, bars and shops. You can find everything from local cuisine to international dishes, from traditional souvenirs to trendy fashion.

The marina is another attraction of Santa Eulàlia. It is one of the most modern and luxurious in Ibiza, with more than 700 moorings for boats of different sizes. The marina also has a yacht club, a sailing school, a diving centre and a fishing club. You can take a boat trip to explore the nearby coves and islands, or enjoy a sunset cruise with music and drinks.

Santa Eulàlia is not only a beach resort, but also a town with a rich history. You can visit the old town, which is located on a hill overlooking the sea. Here you can see the church of Es Puig de Missa, which dates back to the 16th century and has a distinctive fortified appearance. The church also houses a museum of sacred art, where you can admire paintings, sculptures and relics.

Next to the church, you can find the Ethnographic Museum of Ibiza, which is located in a typical farmhouse called Can Ros. The museum displays objects and tools that illustrate the rural life and traditions of Ibiza in the past. You can learn about the agriculture, crafts, clothing, festivals and customs of the islanders.

Santa Eulàlia also has a vibrant cultural scene, with many events and performances throughout the year. You can catch some concerts, festivals or exhibitions in the town hall, the cultural centre or the theatre. You can also enjoy some live music in some of the bars and pubs on the promenade or in the marina.

Santa Eulàlia is a perfect destination for those who want to experience a different side of Ibiza, away from the crowds and noise of other resorts. Santa Eulàlia will make you feel at home with its friendly atmosphere and its charming character.

Puig de Missa: the hilltop church and museum

If you want to discover the historical and cultural heritage of Ibiza, you should not miss Puig de Missa, a picturesque ensemble of buildings on a hill overlooking the town of Santa Eulàlia. Puig de Missa means "hill of the mass" and refers to the church that crowns the hill, which is one of the most outstanding examples of fortified churches in Ibiza and Formentera.

The church of Puig de Missa was built in the 16th and 17th centuries on the ruins of a previous temple that collapsed after a pirate raid. The church has a distinctive appearance, with a nave and a tower that were originally designed to protect the population from attacks. The church also has a beautiful porch with arches and a roof made of sabina wood, a typical material of Ibiza. The interior of the church is simple but elegant, with a baroque style and some paintings, sculptures and relics.

Next to the church, you can visit the Barrau Museum, which is dedicated to the Catalan painter Laureà Barrau, who lived in Ibiza from 1912 to 19572. The museum is located in a charming house with blue doors and windows, and displays some of the works of Barrau, who was inspired by the landscapes and people of Ibiza. You can admire his paintings, drawings and sketches, as well as some personal objects and documents.

A few steps away from the church, you can find the Museum of Ethnography, which is housed in a typical farmhouse called Can Ros. The museum shows the rural life and traditions of Ibiza in the past, through objects and tools related to agriculture, crafts, clothing, festivals and customs. You can learn about the history of the islanders, as well as see some demonstrations of traditional activities such as pottery or basketry.

Puig de Missa is not only a place to visit, but also a place to enjoy. You can walk around its narrow streets and alleys, admiring the white walls of the houses, the colorful flowers and plants, and the crosses that mark the corners. You can also take in the stunning views of Santa Eulàlia and the sea from different points on the hill. You can feel the tranquility and charm of this place, which has been recognized as a picturesque landscape since 1952.

Es Canar: the hippy market and resort

If you are looking for a fun and lively destination in Ibiza, you might want to visit Es Canar, a small resort on the east coast of the island, with a crescent-shaped sandy beach, a small harbour for fishing boats, and home to the largest weekly hippy market.

The resort of Es Canar has a lot to offer to its visitors, from its friendly hotels and apartments to its great choice of bars and restaurants. You can find everything from local cuisine to international dishes, from traditional souvenirs to trendy fashion. You can also enjoy some live music in some of the bars and pubs on the beach or in the harbour. You can also catch some cultural events such as concerts, festivals or exhibitions in nearby towns.

The highlight of Es Canar is the hippy market of Punta Arabi, which takes place every Wednesday from April to October. This is the largest and oldest hippy market in Ibiza, with more than 500 stalls selling various items ranging from jewellery and handbags to rugs and homeware. You can also find local products, handicrafts, clothes, art and more. The market is also a great place to experience the bohemian vibe and the live music of Ibiza. You can listen to bands, singers and DJs playing different genres of music, from rock and pop to reggae and chill-out.

Cala Nova: the surfers' beach

If you are looking for a thrilling and adventurous destination in Ibiza, you might want to visit Cala Nova, a long and wide beach on the east coast of the island, with fine white sand and clear blue water. Cala Nova is one of the few beaches in Ibiza where you can enjoy some decent surf, especially with the right wind conditions.

Cala Nova's beach is one of the most attractive in Ibiza, with a natural and unspoilt scenery, surrounded by pine trees and dunes. The water in Cala Nova is especially clear and transparent, and shimmers in different shades of blue and turquoise. There are quite a few fish to be seen, and the rocky coast to the left is very nice for snorkelling. However, you should be careful when swimming or letting young ones swim in Cala Nova, as there are no buoys to mark off the safe swimming zone on this beach, and there can be strong currents and waves.

The highlight of Cala Nova is the surf, which attracts many locals and visitors who want to experience the thrill of riding the waves. Cala Nova is one of Ibiza's few beaches with decent surf, especially with the right wind conditions. The best time to surf in Cala Nova is from October to April, when the wind blows from the north or northeast. You can rent surfboards or take surf lessons at the beach.

Cala Nova has a lot to offer to its visitors, from its friendly hotels and bungalows to its great choice of bars and restaurants. You can also enjoy some live music in some of the bars and restaurants on the beach or in the nearby resort of Es Canar. You can also catch some cultural events such as concerts, festivals or exhibitions in nearby towns.

Cala Llenya: the pine-fringed cove

If you are looking for a natural and serene destination in Ibiza, you might want to visit Cala Llenya, a small cove on the east coast of the island, with fine white sand and clear blue water. Cala Llenya is surrounded by a lush pine forest, ideal for sheltering from the summer sun or enjoying a picnic.

The water in Cala Llenya is especially clear and transparent, and shimmers in different shades of blue and turquoise. There are quite a few fish to be seen, and the rocky coast to the right is very nice for snorkelling. However, you should be careful when swimming or letting young ones swim in Cala Llenya, as there are no buoys to mark off the safe swimming zone on this beach, and there can be strong currents and waves.

The highlight of Cala Llenya is the pine forest that surrounds it, which gives it a natural and peaceful atmosphere. You can walk around its paths and trails, admiring the greenery and the fragrance of the pines. You can also find some shaded areas where you can rest or have a picnic. You can feel the tranquility and charm of this place, which has been recognized as a natural area of special interest.

Cala Mastella: the rustic beach and restaurant

If you are looking for a unique and authentic destination

in Ibiza, you might want to visit Cala Mastella, a small cove on the east coast of the island, with fine white sand and clear blue water. Cala Mastella is surrounded by pine trees and reeds, and has a charming fishing port with several cabins. Cala Mastella is also home to one of the most famous and legendary restaurants in Ibiza: El Bigotes.

Cala Mastella's beach is one of the most attractive in Ibiza, with a natural and unspoilt scenery, hidden in a small inlet between rocky formations. The water in Cala Mastella is especially clear and transparent, and also shimmers in different shades of blue and turquoise.

The highlight of Cala Mastella is the restaurant El Bigotes, which is also known as Cala Mastella. This is one of the most picturesque, authentic and essential establishments on the island. El Bigotes is run by Juan Ferrer, a former fisherman who started cooking his catch on a fire on the beach in the 1970s. Since then, he has become a legend in Ibiza, attracting celebrities, locals and tourists who want to taste his famous bullit de peix (fish stew) and arroz a banda (rice with fish broth).

El Bigotes is located on a wooden platform over the

water, next to the fishing port. It has a rustic and simple decor, with wooden tables and chairs, fishing nets and photos of famous guests. The menu is based on fresh fish and seafood, cooked in a traditional way. The most popular dishes are the bullit de peix and the arroz a banda, which are served at 2 pm and 4 pm respectively. You can also order grilled fish or squid, salads, bread with aioli (garlic sauce) and sangria.

El Bigotes is open from April to October, from 12 pm to 6 pm. It is advisable to book in advance, as it is very busy and there are limited seats. You can reach El Bigotes by boat from Santa Eulàlia or Es Canar.

You can find accommodation options for every taste and budget in nearby towns such as Sant Carles de Peralta or Es Canar. You can also rent a car or a bike to explore other attractions on the east coast or on the island. Cala Mastella will make you feel enchanted with its beauty.

Recommendations for Accommodation

If you are looking for accommodation in Santa Eulalia and East Coast, you have a wide range of options to choose from. You can find hotels, apartments, villas, hostels, and campsites that cater to different needs and preferences. Below are some of the best accommodation in Santa Eulalia and East Coast that we recommend:

Oda | Ibiza, Spain: This is a website that allows you to search and book properties for your stay in Ibiza. You can filter by location, price, rating, facilities, and more. You can also read reviews from other travelers and see photos of the properties. Oda offers some of the best deals and discounts for accommodation in Santa Eulalia and East Coast.

Aguas de Ibiza Grand Luxe Hotel: This is a 5-star hotel located on the seafront near Santa Eulalia, where you can enjoy a luxurious and eco-friendly experience. Aguas de Ibiza has 145 rooms and suites with balconies, air conditioning, satellite TV, minibar, safe, free WiFi, and private bathroom. It also has an outdoor pool with sun loungers, a spa with thermal circuit and treatments, a restaurant with Mediterranean cuisine, a bar with cocktails and music, and a 24-hour reception. Aguas de Ibiza is a premium hotel that offers excellent service and facilities.

Invisa Hotel La Cala: This is a 4-star hotel located in the center of Santa Eulalia, close to the beach and the marina. Invisa Hotel La Cala has 180 rooms with balconies, air conditioning, satellite TV, free WiFi, safe, and private bathroom. It also has an outdoor pool with sun loungers, a restaurant with buffet service, a bar with snacks and drinks, a wellness center with sauna and jacuzzi, and a 24-hour reception. Invisa Hotel La Cala is a modern and comfortable hotel that offers high-quality service and facilities.

Apartamentos Parot Quality: This is an apartment complex located in the center of Santa Eulalia, close to the beach and the shops. Apartamentos Parot Quality has 24 apartments with balconies, air conditioning, satellite TV, kitchenette, coffee machine, free WiFi, safe, and private bathroom. It also has a terrace with views of the town, a restaurant with local cuisine, and free parking. Apartamentos Parot Quality is a cozy and convenient apartment complex that offers spacious and well-equipped apartments.

Camping La Playa Ibiza: This is a campsite located on the beachfront near Es Canar, where you can enjoy a natural and authentic experience. Camping La Playa Ibiza has 50 pitches with electricity, water, and drainage. It also has bungalows with air conditioning, TV, kitchenette, free WiFi, and private bathroom. It also has a swimming pool with sun loungers, a restaurant with pizza and barbecue, a bar with drinks and music, and free parking. Camping La Playa Ibiza is a charming and friendly campsite that offers relaxing and affordable accommodation.

Recommendations for Restaurants

If you are looking for restaurants in Santa Eulalia and East Coast, you have a wide range of options to choose from. You can find restaurants that offer local and international cuisine, with fresh seafood, grilled meat, salads, paellas, pizzas, sushi, and more. You can also find restaurants that offer different settings and atmospheres, such as beachfront, countryside, terrace, or rooftop. Below are some of the best restaurants in Santa Eulalia and East Coast that we recommend:

La Mar de Santa: This is a restaurant located on the beachfront of Santa Eulalia, near the Congress Hall. It offers high-quality Mediterranean cuisine with a local touch in a peaceful setting beside the sea. You can enjoy dishes such as gazpacho, seafood rice, grilled fish, or almond cake. You can also enjoy views of the sea and the nearby islands from the terrace.

Royal India: This is a restaurant located in the center

of Santa Eulalia, near the marina. It offers authentic Indian cuisine with a variety of dishes, such as curry, tandoori, biryani, or naan bread. You can also enjoy drinks such as lassi or chai. Royal India is a restaurant that offers excellent service and quality.

Can Carlos: This is a restaurant located in the center of Santa Gertrudis, a charming village in the interior of the island. It offers Italian cuisine with a creative twist, such as burrata salad, truffle pasta, sea bass fillet, or tiramisu. You can also enjoy views of the town and the church from the terrace.

Es Terral: This is a restaurant located on the beachfront of Es Figueral, near Es Canar. It offers French cuisine with fresh and organic ingredients, such as scallop carpaccio, duck breast, or chocolate soufflé. You can also enjoy views of the sea and Es Vedrà island from the terrace. Es Terral is a restaurant that offers a charming and romantic experience.

Wild Beets: This is a restaurant located in the center of Santa Gertrudis, near Can Carlos. It offers vegan cuisine with raw-food, gluten-free and wild-bowl options, such as gazpacho, quinoa salad, veggie burger, or chocolate cake. You can also enjoy drinks such as smoothies and detox drinks. Wild Beets is a restaurant that offers high-quality service and food.

North Coast and Interior

If you want to escape the hustle and bustle of the south and discover the most authentic and natural side of Ibiza, you should head to the north coast and interior of the island. This area is the least populated and most rural part of Ibiza, with a bohemian and off-grid vibe thanks to its strong hippy heritage and spectacular, remote landscapes.

The north coast of Ibiza has some of the most beautiful and secluded beaches on the island, ranging from long and wide sandy bays to small and hidden coves. Some of the most popular ones are Portinatx, Benirràs, Cala Nova, Cala Llenya, Cala Mastella and Es Figueral. You can relax on the soft sand, swim in the clear water, or try some water sports such as surfing, kayaking or sailing. You can also take a boat trip to explore the nearby islands of Tagomago or Es Vedrà.

The interior of Ibiza is a magical place of forested hills, twisting backroads, timeworn whitewashed villages and ancient churches. You can explore the charming towns of Sant Joan, Sant Carles, Sant Llorenç and Santa Gertrudis, where you can experience the low-key Ibizan life and culture. You can also visit some historical and cultural attractions such as the cave of Cova des Culleram, the fortified church of Sant Miquel, the farmhouse of Es Trull de Ca n'Andreu or the lighthouse of Far de Portinatx.

The north coast and interior of Ibiza are also ideal for outdoor activities such as cycling, hiking or horse riding. You can enjoy the stunning views of the sea and the countryside, as well as the flora and fauna of the island. You can find some marked trails and routes that will take you to some scenic spots such as Puig de Missa, Balàfia, Torre d'en Valls or Port de Ses Caletes. You can also join some guided tours or rent a bike or a horse to explore the area at your own pace.

One of the main attractions of the north coast and interior of Ibiza is the hippy market of Punta Arabi in Es Canar, which takes place every Wednesday from April to October. This is the largest and oldest hippy market in Ibiza, with more than 500 stalls selling various items ranging from jewellery and handbags to rugs and homeware. You can also find local products, handicrafts, clothes, art and more. The market is also a great place to experience the bohemian vibe and the live music of Ibiza.

The north coast and interior of Ibiza are not known for their nightlife, but they do have some bars and pubs where you can have a drink and listen to some music.

Sant Joan: the sleepy village

If you want to experience the most authentic and tranquil side of Ibiza, you should visit Sant Joan, a sleepy village in the north of the island, with a traditional and rural charm. Sant Joan (Sant Joan de Labritja in Catalan) is the main town of the municipality of the same name, which covers the northernmost part of Ibiza.

Sant Joan's main attraction is its 18th century whitewashed church, which dominates the village square. The church has a fortified appearance, with a nave and a tower that were originally designed to protect the population from pirate attacks. The church also has a beautiful porch with arches and a roof made of sabina wood, a typical material of Ibiza. The interior of the church is simple but elegant, with a baroque style and some paintings, sculptures and relics.

The village square is a pleasant and quiet place where you can enjoy a stroll or a coffee, admiring the flowers and the ancient wooden doors that lead to the cobbled streets and alleys. The square also hosts some cultural events throughout the year, such as concerts, festivals or exhibitions. One of the most popular ones is the Fiesta de Sant Joan on June 23rd and 24th, celebrating Saint John the Baptist, the patron saint of Sant Joan. The fiesta features fireworks, bonfires, music and dancing. Sant Joan is also close to some stunning beaches such as Portinatx, Benirràs, Cala Nova, Cala Llenya or Cala Mastella.

Portinatx: the secluded bay and lighthouse

If you are looking for a quiet and scenic destination in Ibiza, you might want to visit Portinatx, a secluded bay on the north coast of the island, with fine white sand and clear blue water. Portinatx is surrounded by pine trees and cliffs, and has a small harbour for fishing boats. Portinatx is also home to the tallest lighthouse in the

Balearic Islands: the Far de Portinatx.

The highlight of Portinatx is the lighthouse of Far de Portinatx, which stands on a hill overlooking the bay. The lighthouse was built in 1977 to provide safety to the navigation in the north of Ibiza, as there was no other light signal between the lighthouse of Tagomago (in the east) and the one of Sa Conillera (in the west). The lighthouse is 52 metres high and has a range of 23 nautical miles. It is not open to the public, but you can admire it from a distance or take a walk to its base.

Sant Miquel: the cave and beach

Sant Miquel (Sant Joan de Labritja in Catalan) is the main town of the municipality of the same name, which covers the northernmost part of Ibiza. Sant Miquel has two main attractions: its 18th century whitewashed church and its nearby cave of Can Marça.

Sant Miquel's cave is called Can Marça and is located high above the beach of Puerto de San Miguel, which was once the fishing port of Sant Miquel. The cave is a former smugglers' hideaway, where they used to store their goods and mark their routes with signs. The cave has been restored and opened to the public, with guided tours through its chambers, galleries and tunnels. You can see some fascinating stalactite and stalagmite formations, as well as an underground waterfall that is illuminated by different colours.

The beach of Puerto de San Miguel is one of the most attractive in Ibiza, with fine white sand and clear blue water. It is ideal for families, couples and anyone who wants to enjoy a relaxing day by the sea. The beach has all the facilities and services you need, such as sunbeds, umbrellas, showers, lifeguards, water sports and boat rentals. You can also take a boat trip to explore the nearby coves and islands, or enjoy a sunset cruise with music and drinks.

Sant Llorenç: the rural charm

Sant Llorenç (Sant Joan de Labritja in Catalan) is the main town of the municipality of the same name, which covers the northernmost part of Ibiza. Sant Llorenç's main attraction is its 18th century whitewashed church, which dominates the village square. The church has a beautiful porch with arches and a roof made of sabina wood, a typical material of Ibiza.

Sant Llorenç is not only a village, but also a gateway to explore the north coast and interior of Ibiza, which offer some of the most beautiful and natural landscapes on the island. You can visit some charming towns such as Sant Joan, Sant Carles or Santa Gertrudis, where you can experience the low-key Ibizan life and culture. You can also visit some historical and cultural attractions such as the cave of Cova des Culleram, the fortified church of Sant Miquel, the farmhouse of Es Trull de Ca n'Andreu or the lighthouse of Far de Portinatx.

Sant Llorenç is also close to some stunning beaches such as Portinatx, Benirràs, Cala Nova, Cala Llenya or Cala Mastella.

Santa Gertrudis: the gastronomic hub

If you are looking for a delicious and diverse destination in Ibiza, you might want to visit Santa Gertrudis, a charming village in the heart of the island, with a wide choice of restaurants and bars, offering everything from gourmet cuisine to rustic local bars. Santa Gertrudis (Santa Gertrudis de Fruitera in Catalan) is the main town of the municipality of the same name, which covers the northernmost part of Ibiza.

Santa Gertrudis's main attraction is its gastronomy, which reflects the varied culture of the island. You can find everything from traditional Ibizan dishes such as sofrit pagès (a stew of meat and potatoes) or flaó (a cheese and mint cake) to international specialties such as sushi, pizza or burgers. You can also taste some local products such as honey, cheese, wine or herbs.

The village square is a lively and cozy place where you can enjoy a meal or a drink, surrounded by a cluster of bars, restaurants and shops. The square is also a pedestrian-friendly plaza where hip café bars and restaurants have joined traditional Ibicenco establishments. The atmosphere of the village is traditional, but also modern and sophisticated.

Some of the most popular and famous places to eat and drink in Santa Gertrudis are:

Bar Costa: This is one of the oldest and most iconic bars in Ibiza, where penniless artists in the hippy era would swap paintings for food and now oil paintings compete with the restaurant's famous hams for hanging space. You can enjoy some tasty tapas, sandwiches and salads, as well as some local wine or beer.

Bistro Plaza: This is a chic and elegant restaurant that offers a fusion of Mediterranean and Asian cuisine, with dishes such as tuna tartare, duck confit or Thai curry. You can also enjoy some cocktails, wines or champagnes on its terrace overlooking the square.

Es Canto: This is a cozy and rustic restaurant that specializes in Ibizan cuisine, with dishes such as bullit de peix (fish stew), arroz de matanzas (rice with pork) or greixonera (a pudding made with bread and eggs). You can also try some homemade desserts such as flan or almond cake.

Macao Café: This is a trendy and stylish restaurant that offers a fusion of Italian and Asian cuisine, with dishes such as pasta, pizza, sushi or dim sum. You can also enjoy some live music and DJ sets on its terrace or in its lounge bar.

Musset: This is a modern and healthy café that offers a variety of organic and vegetarian options, such as salads, sandwiches, wraps or smoothies. You can also enjoy some cakes, pastries or coffee on its terrace or in its cozy interior.

Santa Gertrudis is not only a gastronomic hub, but also a

gateway to explore the north coast and interior of Ibiza. You can visit some charming towns such as Sant Joan, Sant Carles or Sant Llorenç, where you can experience the low-key Ibizan life and culture. You can also visit some historical and cultural attractions such as the cave of Cova des Culleram, the fortified church of Sant Miquel, the farmhouse of Es Trull de Ca n'Andreu or the lighthouse of Far de Portinatx.

Sant Rafel: the pottery town

If you want to discover the most artistic and crafty side of Ibiza, you should visit Sant Rafel, a small village on the main road between Ibiza Town and San Antonio, with a long tradition of pottery and ceramics. Sant Rafel (Sant Rafel de sa Creu in Catalan) is the main town of the municipality of the same name, which covers the central part of Ibiza.

Sant Rafel's main attraction is its pottery workshops, which have been declared the only artisan zone – Zona de Interés Artesanal – on Ibiza because of the traditional pottery shops there. You can see how the local potters create beautiful handmade ceramics and pottery, using techniques and materials that have been passed down for generations. You can also buy some unique pieces, such as plates, bowls, vases, jugs or lamps, in different shapes, colours and designs.

The village square is a pleasant and quiet place where you can enjoy a stroll or a coffee, admiring the flowers and the ancient wooden doors that lead to the cobbled streets and alleys. The square also hosts some cultural events throughout the year, such as concerts, festivals or exhibitions. One of the most popular ones is the Fiesta de Sant Rafel on October 24th, celebrating Saint Raphael, the patron saint of Sant Rafel. The fiesta features fireworks, music and dancing.

Recommendations for Accommodation

If you are looking for accommodation in North Coast and Interior, you have a wide range of options to choose from. You can find hotels, apartments, villas, hostels, and campsites that cater to different needs and preferences. Below are some of the best accommodation in North Coast and Interior that we recommend:

Atzaró: This is a 5-star hotel located in the countryside near Santa Eulalia, where you can enjoy a luxurious and eco-friendly experience. Atzaró has 25 rooms and suites with balconies, air conditioning, satellite TV, minibar, safe, free WiFi, and private bathroom. It also has an outdoor pool with sun loungers, a spa with thermal circuit and treatments, a restaurant with Mediterranean cuisine, a bar with cocktails and music, and a 24-hour reception. Atzaró is a premium hotel that offers excellent service and facilities.

Can Pujolet: This is a 4-star hotel located in the countryside near Santa Agnès, where you can enjoy a natural and authentic experience. Can Pujolet has 10 rooms with air conditioning, satellite TV, free WiFi, safe, and private bathroom. It also has an outdoor pool with sun loungers, a restaurant with local cuisine, a massage area, and free parking. Can Pujolet is a charming country house that offers relaxing and affordable accommodation.

Los Enamorados: This is a 4-star hotel located on the seafront near Portinatx, where you can enjoy a romantic and bohemian experience. Los Enamorados has 9 rooms with balconies, air conditioning, satellite TV, minibar, safe, free WiFi, and private bathroom. It also has a terrace with views of the sea, a restaurant with fusion cuisine, a bar with cocktails and music, and a boutique with clothing and accessories. Los Enamorados is a stylish and lively hotel that offers high-quality service and facilities.

Camping La Playa Ibiza: This is a campsite located on the beachfront near Es Figueral, where you can enjoy a natural and authentic experience. Camping La Playa Ibiza has 50 pitches with electricity, water, and drainage. It also has bungalows with air conditioning, TV, kitchenette, free WiFi, and private bathroom. It also has a swimming pool with sun loungers, a restaurant with pizza and barbecue, a bar with drinks and music, and free parking. Camping La Playa Ibiza is a charming and friendly campsite that offers relaxing and affordable accommodation.

Recommendations for Restaurants

If you are looking for restaurants in North Coast and Interior, you have a wide range of options to choose from. You can find restaurants that offer local and international cuisine, with fresh seafood, grilled meat, salads, paellas, pizzas, sushi, and more. You can also find restaurants that offer different settings and atmospheres, such as beachfront, countryside, terrace, or rooftop. Below are some of the best restaurants in

North Coast and Interior that we recommend:

Giri Café: This is a restaurant located in the center of San Juan, a picturesque village in the north of the island. It has an exquisitely stylish rustic-chic interior and a blissful garden. It offers progressive foodie dishes with organic and local ingredients, such as tuna tartare, octopus salad, lamb chops, or cheesecake. It also has a bar with cocktails and music. Giri Café is a restaurant that offers excellent service and quality.

Wild Beets: This is a restaurant located in the center of Santa Gertrudis, a charming village in the interior of the island. It has a cozy and intimate atmosphere with wooden tables and cushions. It offers vegan cuisine with raw-food, gluten-free and wild-bowl options, such as gazpacho, quinoa salad, veggie burger, or chocolate cake. It also has a juice bar with smoothies and detox drinks. Wild Beets is a restaurant that offers high-quality service and food.

La Paloma: This is a restaurant located in the countryside near San Lorenzo, surrounded by lush gardens. It has a boho-chic decoration with white walls and furniture, colorful paintings, and candles. It offers Italian cuisine with a creative twist, such as burrata salad, truffle pasta, sea bass fillet, or tiramisu. It also has a terrace with views of the garden and the church. La Paloma is a restaurant that offers charming and romantic experience.

Los Enamorados: This is a restaurant located on the seafront near Portinatx, where you can enjoy stunning views of the sea and the cliffs. It has a Cuban-inspired design and atmosphere, with wooden tables and chairs, cushions, and neon lights. It offers Japanese and Peruvian fusion cuisine with fresh Ibizan seafood, such as scallop carpaccio, ceviche, sushi, or miso cod. It also has a bar with cocktails and music, and a boutique with clothing and accessories. Los Enamorados is a stylish and lively restaurant that offers high-quality service and facilities.

Ses Escoles: This is a restaurant located on the main road near San Lorenzo, in an old olive-oil estate that dates back to the 18th century. It has been renovated with respect for its history and architecture. It offers Mediterranean cuisine with local products, such as gazpacho, seafood rice, grilled fish, or almond cake. It also has a wine cellar with more than 200 references, and an oleoteca (olive-oil tasting room) where you can buy Ibizan cheeses and oils. Ses Escoles is a restaurant that offers a luxurious and exclusive experience.

Formentera

If you are looking for a peaceful and natural destination in the Mediterranean Sea, you might want to visit Formentera, the smallest and most southerly island of the Pityusic Islands group, which belongs to the Balearic Islands autonomous community of Spain. Formentera covers an area of 83.22 square kilometres (32.13 sq mi) and has a population of 12,111 as of 2019.

Formentera's name is usually said to derive from the Latin word frumentarium, meaning "granary", as the island was used to store grain in ancient times. The island has a rich history, having been occupied by various civilizations such as the Carthaginians, the Romans, the Byzantines, the Arabs, the Norwegians, the Catalans and the Spanish. The island was also a refuge for hippies and artists in the 1960s and 1970s, who left their mark on its culture and lifestyle.

Formentera's main attraction is its beaches, which are considered some of the most beautiful and pristine in Europe. The island has more than 20 kilometres (12 mi) of coastline, with fine white sand and clear turquoise water. Some of the most popular beaches are Ses Illetes,

Es Pujols, Cala Saona, Migjorn and Es Caló. You can relax on the sunbeds, swim in the sea, or try some water sports such as sailing, windsurfing or diving. You can also take a boat trip to explore the nearby islets such as Espalmador or S'Espardell.

Formentera is also known for its natural and rural scenery, which has been preserved thanks to its environmental policies and its status as a natural area of special interest. The island has a varied landscape of hills, valleys, forests, fields and salt flats. You can enjoy the views of the sea and the countryside from various points such as La Mola lighthouse, Cap de Barbaria or Es Ram. You can also admire the flora and fauna of the island, such as pine trees, junipers, orchids, lizards and birds.

Formentera is not only a beach resort, but also a cultural and gastronomic destination. You can visit some charming villages such as Sant Francesc Xavier, Sant Ferran de ses Roques or El Pilar de la Mola, where you can see some historical and artistic monuments such as churches, museums or art galleries. You can also taste some local dishes such as bullit de peix (fish stew), arroz a banda (rice with fish broth) or flaó (cheese and mint cake). You can also enjoy some live music and nightlife in some of the bars and clubs on the island.

Formentera is a perfect destination for those who want to enjoy a relaxing holiday with a touch of nature and culture in the Mediterranean Sea. You can find accommodation options for every budget and preference, from luxury hotels to cozy apartments. You can also rent a car or a bike to explore the island at your own pace. You can reach Formentera by ferry from Ibiza or by plane from other Spanish or European cities. Formentera will make you feel at ease with its friendly atmosphere and its stunning character.

How to get there and around

Formentera is the smallest and most southerly island of the Pityuses, a group of islands that belongs to the Balearic Islands autonomous community of Spain. Formentera is known for its peaceful and natural beauty, with stunning beaches, rural scenery and cultural attractions. If you want to visit this island paradise, below are some tips on how to get there and how to move around.

Getting to Formentera

Formentera does not have an airport, so the only way to reach it is by sea. The island's only entry and exit point is the port of La Savina, where you can find various ferry companies that connect Formentera with Ibiza and mainland Spain.

From Ibiza: The most common and convenient way to get to Formentera is by taking a ferry from Ibiza, which is only 30 minutes away by boat. You can catch a flight to Ibiza Airport from many Spanish and European cities, and then take a bus or a taxi to the ferry terminal in Ibiza Town. There are several ferry companies that operate regular crossings from Ibiza to Formentera, such as Med Pitiusa, Trasmapi, Baleària and Aquabus. You can book your ferry tickets online or buy them at the port. The ferry schedule varies depending on the season and the demand, but you can usually find departures every hour or half an hour from 6 am to 10 pm.

From mainland Spain: Another option to get to Formentera is by taking a direct ferry from mainland Spain, which can take from 2 to 4 hours depending on the route and the speed of the boat. You can choose from several ports such as Dénia, Valencia or Barcelona, where you can find ferry companies such as Baleària or Trasmediterranea. You can book your ferry tickets online or buy them at the port. The ferry schedule varies depending on the season and the demand, but you can usually find departures every day or every week.

Getting around Formentera

Once you arrive in Formentera, you have several options to move around the island, depending on your preferences and budget. The island is small and flat, so it is easy to explore by bike, bus, scooter or car. You can also find electric versions of most of these vehicles, which are more eco-friendly and help to preserve the island's environment.

By bike: One of the best ways to get around Formentera is by bike, which allows you to enjoy the island's natural beauty and discover its hidden gems. The island has an excellent network of 32 'green routes' of rural paths and tracks that connect the main towns and beaches. You can rent a bike or an electric bike in La Savina or from other specialists around the island. You can also join a guided tour or rent an audio guide to learn more about the island's history and culture.

By bus: Another option to get around Formentera is by bus, which is cheap and convenient for longer or more tiring journeys. The island has four bus routes (L1, L2, L5 & L7) that operate throughout the year, with increased frequency during the summer months. There is also a night bus (N6) and a minibus adapted for people with special mobility needs. The buses cover most of the key towns and beaches on the island, such as Sant Francesc Xavier, Sant Ferran de ses Roques, El Pilar de la Mola, Es Pujols, Ses Illetes or Cala Saona.

By scooter: Another option to get around Formentera is by scooter, which is fun and fast for shorter distances. The scooter is also ideal for exploring some of the more remote parts of the island that are not accessible by car or bus. You can rent a scooter or an electric scooter in La Savina or from other specialists around the island. You need a valid driving license and a helmet to drive a scooter on Formentera.

By car: Another option to get around Formentera is by car, which gives you more comfort and flexibility for longer trips or if you are travelling with your family or friends. The car also allows you to carry more luggage or equipment for your activities on the island. You can rent a car or an electric car in La Savina or from other specialists around the island. You need a valid driving license and insurance to drive a car on Formentera.

By boat: Another option to get around Formentera is by boat, which gives you a different perspective of the island's coastline and its nearby islets. The boat also allows you to access some of the more secluded beaches and coves that are not reachable by land. You can rent a boat or take a boat trip in La Savina or from other specialists around the island. You can also find some sea taxis that offer boat transfers between Ibiza and Formentera.

La Savina: the port and salt flats

If you want to visit Formentera, the smallest and most southerly island of the Pityuses, you will have to pass through La Savina, the only port and entry point of the island. La Savina is a small town on the north coast of Formentera, with a working harbour, a marina and a nautical atmosphere. La Savina is also close to the Las Salinas salt flats, a natural and historical attraction of the island.

La Savina's port is where all the ferries from Ibiza and mainland Spain arrive and depart. You can find various ferry companies that offer regular crossings, such as Med Pitiusa, Trasmapi, Baleària and Aquabus. You can book your ferry tickets online or buy them at the port. The ferry schedule varies depending on the season and the demand, but you can usually find departures every hour or half an hour from 6 am to 10 pm2. The port also has a harbour building where you can find a bar, a shop and some tourist information.

La Savina's marina is where many yachts and boats come to moor, especially in summer. You can admire the impressive vessels and the sea views from the promenade or the pier. You can also rent a boat or take a boat trip to explore the nearby beaches and islands, such as Espalmador or S'Espardell. You can also find some sea taxis that offer boat transfers between Ibiza and Formentera.

La Savina's town is where you can find some bars, cafes, restaurants and shops, as well as some bike, scooter and car rental places. You can enjoy a meal or a drink overlooking the harbour or the salt flats. You can also buy some souvenirs or local products, such as honey, cheese, wine or herbs. In summer, there are also some market stalls selling clothing, jewellery, handicrafts and more.

La Savina's salt flats are located east of the town, near the road that leads to Sant Francesc Xavier. They are part of the Ses Salines Natural Park, which covers both Formentera and Ibiza. The salt flats have been used since ancient times to produce salt, which was an important source of income and trade for the islanders. The salt flats are also home to many birds, such as flamingos, herons and gulls. You can walk around the salt flats or take a guided tour to learn more about their history and ecology.

La Savina is a perfect destination for those who want to start or end their visit to Formentera. You can find accommodation options for every budget and preference, from luxury hotels to cozy apartments. You can also rent a car or a bike to explore other attractions on the island. La Savina will make you feel welcome with its friendly atmosphere and its stunning character.

Sant Francesc: the capital and church square

If you want to discover the most historical and cultural side of Formentera, you should visit Sant Francesc, the capital and largest town of the island, with a charming and lively church square. Sant Francesc (Sant Francesc Xavier in Catalan) is the main town of the municipality of the same name, which covers the central part of Formentera.

Sant Francesc's main attraction is its 18th century whitewashed church, which stands on the main square of the town. The church was built between 1726 and 1738 by the state, as Formentera did not have a bishopric or a parish at that time. The church has a simple and austere appearance, with a nave and a bell tower. The church also has a beautiful porch with arches and a roof made of sabina wood, a typical material of Formentera. The interior of the church is decorated with paintings, sculptures and altarpieces.

The church square is a lively and cozy place where you can enjoy a stroll or a coffee, surrounded by bars, cafes, restaurants and shops. The square is also a pedestrian-friendly area where you can see some street art and performances. The square also hosts some cultural events throughout the year, such as concerts, festivals or exhibitions1. One of the most popular ones is the Fiesta de Sant Francesc on December 3rd, celebrating Saint Francis Xavier, the patron saint of Sant Francesc. The fiesta features fireworks, music and dancing.

Sant Francesc is not only a historical and cultural hub, but also a gateway to explore other attractions on the island. You can visit some charming villages such as Sant Ferran de ses Roques, El Pilar de la Mola or La Savina, where you can see some historical and artistic monuments such as churches, museums or art galleries1. You can also visit some natural and rural attractions such as the Las Salinas salt flats, the Ses Illetes beach or the Es Ram hill.

Illetes: the Caribbean-like beach

If you are looking for a stunning and paradisiacal destination in the Mediterranean Sea, you might want to visit Illetes, a beach on the north coast of Formentera, the smallest and most southerly island of the Pityuses. Illetes (Ses Illetes in Catalan) is part of the Natural Park of Ses Salines de Eivissa and Formentera, a protected area that covers both Formentera and Ibiza.

Illetes's main attraction is its beach, which has been declared one of the most beautiful beaches in the world on more than one occasion. The beach is located on the Es Trucadors peninsula, the northernmost tip of Formentera, and faces west. There are more than 450 metres of beach divided into two parts by a small rocky area in the middle. Its name refers to several islets that lie off this stretch of coast and which are known by the names of: Illa de Tramuntana, Illa des Forn, Escull des Pou, Illa Redona and Escull d'en Palla. Their presence makes the landscape of this beach even more unique.

The most outstanding feature of this beach is its calm, shallow, turquoise waters, which, together with the fine white sand, create a Caribbean-like scenery. The water is so clear and transparent that you can see the bottom and the fish swimming around. The rocky coast to the right is very nice for snorkelling, as you can find some coral and marine life. However, you should be careful when swimming or letting young ones swim in Illetes, as there are no buoys to mark off the safe swimming zone on this beach, and there can be strong currents and waves.

Illetes has all the facilities and services you need to enjoy a relaxing day by the sea, such as sunbeds, umbrellas, showers, lifeguards, water sports and boat rentals. You can also find some restaurants and bars along the beach, where you can taste some local cuisine or have a drink with a view. You can also take a boat trip to explore the nearby islands of Espalmador or S'Espardell, or enjoy a sunset cruise with music and drinks.

Illetes is not only a beach resort, but also a gateway to explore other attractions on Formentera. You can visit some charming villages such as Sant Francesc Xavier, Sant Ferran de ses Roques or El Pilar de la Mola, where you can see some historical and artistic monuments such as churches, museums or art galleries. You can also visit some natural and rural attractions such as the Las Salinas salt flats, the Es Ram hill or the La Mola lighthouse.

Es Pujols: the main tourist resort

If you are looking for a lively and fun destination in Formentera, the smallest and most southerly island of the Pityuses, you might want to visit Es Pujols, a small town on the north coast of the island, with a wide range of hotels, restaurants, bars and shops. Es Pujols is the only urban beach on the island, and the main tourist resort of Formentera.

Es Pujols's main attraction is its beach, which is located on a bay facing west. The beach has more than 300 metres of fine white sand and clear blue water. Es

Pujols's town is where you can find some of the best nightlife and entertainment options on Formentera. You can choose from a variety of bars, pubs, clubs and discos, where you can have a drink, listen to some music or dance until dawn. You can also find some live music and performances in some of the venues on the beach or in the harbour. The atmosphere of the town is festive, but also friendly and safe.

Es Pujols's gastronomy is another of its strong points, with a great choice of restaurants and cafes that cater to all tastes and budgets. You can find everything from local cuisine to international dishes, from seafood to pizza. You can also taste some local products such as honey, cheese, wine or herbs. Some of the most popular and famous places to eat and drink in Es Pujols are:

Sa Palmera: This is a traditional and cozy restaurant that specializes in Ibizan cuisine, with dishes such as bullit de peix (fish stew), arroz de matanzas (rice with pork) or flaó (cheese and mint cake). You can also try some homemade desserts such as flan or almond cake.

Chezz Gerdi: This is a chic and trendy restaurant that offers a fusion of Mediterranean and Asian cuisine, with dishes such as tuna tartare, duck confit or Thai curry.

You can also enjoy some cocktails, wines or champagnes on its terrace overlooking the sea.

Casanita Cantina y Pescado: This is a cozy and rustic restaurant that specializes in Italian cuisine, with dishes such as pasta, pizza, risotto or fish. You can also enjoy some local wine or beer on its terrace or in its garden.

Integral: This is a modern and healthy cafe that offers a variety of organic and vegetarian options, such as salads, sandwiches, wraps or smoothies. You can also enjoy some cakes, pastries or coffee on its terrace or in its cozy interior.

La Mola: the lighthouse and market

If you want to discover the most elevated and scenic side of Formentera, the smallest and most southerly island of the Pityuses, you might want to visit La Mola, a plateau on the east coast of the island, with a lighthouse and a market as its main attractions. La Mola (El Pilar de la Mola in Catalan) is the main town of the municipality of the same name, which covers the eastern part of Formentera.

La Mola's lighthouse is located on the edge of a cliff, at

120 metres above sea level, making it the highest point of Formentera. The lighthouse was built in 1861 and has a height of 21 metres. It has a range of 23 nautical miles and flashes every 10 seconds. It is not open to the public, but you can admire it from a distance or take a walk to its base. The lighthouse also offers spectacular views of the sea and the island, especially at sunrise or sunset.

La Mola's market is held twice a week, on Wednesdays and Sundays, from 4 pm to 10 pm, at the main square of the town. The market is also known as the "hippie market", as it has been running since the 1960s, when many hippies and artists settled in Formentera. The market sells a variety of handmade products, such as clothing, jewellery, pottery, paintings and more.

La Mola's town is where you can find some bars, restaurants and shops, as well as some historical and cultural monuments such as churches, museums or art galleries. You can enjoy a meal or a drink overlooking the square or the countryside. You can also buy some souvenirs or local products, such as honey, cheese, wine or herbs1. Some of the most popular and famous places to eat and drink in La Mola are:

Can Toni: This is a traditional and cozy restaurant that specializes in Ibizan cuisine, with dishes such as bullit de peix (fish stew), arroz de matanzas (rice with pork) or flaó (cheese and mint cake). You can also try some homemade desserts such as flan or almond cake.

La Fonda Pepe: This is a historic and iconic restaurant that has been serving since 1972. It offers a fusion of Mediterranean and international cuisine, with dishes such as pasta, pizza, sushi or curry. You can also enjoy some cocktails, wines or beers on its terrace overlooking the square.

Blue Bar: This is a trendy and colourful bar that offers a variety of drinks and snacks, as well as some live music and DJ sets. It is decorated with blue lights and paintings by local artists. You can also enjoy some views of the sea and the island from its rooftop terrace.

Recommendations for Accommodation

If you are looking for accommodation in Formentera, you have a wide range of options to choose from. You can find hotels, apartments, villas, hostels, and campsites that cater to different needs and preferences. Below are some of the best accommodation in

Formentera that we recommend:

Oda | Formentera, Spain: This is a website that allows you to search and book properties for your stay in Formentera. You can filter by location, price, rating, facilities, and more. You can also read reviews from other travelers and see photos of the properties. Oda offers some of the best deals and discounts for accommodation in Formentera.

Hotel Cala Saona & Spa: This is a 4-star hotel located on the beachfront of Cala Saona, one of the most beautiful and natural beaches on the island. It has 99 rooms with balconies, air conditioning, satellite TV, minibar, safe, free WiFi, and private bathroom. It also has an outdoor pool with sun loungers, a spa with thermal circuit and treatments, a restaurant with Mediterranean cuisine, a bar with cocktails and music, and a 24-hour reception. Hotel Cala Saona & Spa is a modern and comfortable hotel that offers high-quality service and facilities.

Apartamentos Paraiso de los Pinos: This is an apartment complex located in the countryside near Es Pujols, the main tourist center of the island. It has 28 apartments with terraces, air conditioning, satellite TV, kitchenette, coffee machine, free WiFi, safe, and private bathroom. It also has an outdoor pool with sun loungers, a restaurant with local cuisine, a bar with drinks and snacks, and free parking. Apartamentos Paraiso de los Pinos is a cozy and convenient apartment complex that offers spacious and well-equipped apartments.

Hostal Casbah: This is a 2-star hotel located in the countryside near Sant Francesc Xavier, the capital of the island. It has 29 rooms with air conditioning, satellite TV, free WiFi, safe, and private bathroom. It also has an outdoor pool with sun loungers, a restaurant with buffet service, a bar with snacks and drinks, and free parking. Hostal Casbah is a charming and friendly hotel that offers relaxing and affordable accommodation.

Camping La Playa Ibiza: This is a campsite located on the beachfront near Es Arenals, where you can enjoy a natural and authentic experience. Camping La Playa Ibiza has 50 pitches with electricity, water, and drainage. It also has bungalows with air conditioning, TV, kitchenette, free WiFi, and private bathroom. It also has a swimming pool with sun loungers, a restaurant with pizza and barbecue, a bar with drinks and music, and free parking. Camping La Playa Ibiza is a charming and friendly campsite that offers relaxing and affordable accommodation.

Recommendations for Restaurants

If you are looking for restaurants in Formentera, you have a wide range of options to choose from. You can find restaurants that offer local and international cuisine, with fresh seafood, grilled meat, salads, paellas, pizzas, sushi, and more. You can also find restaurants that offer different settings and atmospheres, such as beachfront, countryside, terrace, or rooftop. Below are some of the best restaurants in Formentera that we recommend:

Juan y Andrea: This is a restaurant located on the beachfront of Illetes, one of the most beautiful and natural beaches on the island. It has been serving fresh seafood since 1971, such as paella, fideuá, local prawns, lobster, and the famous Raó of Formentera. It also has a terrace with stunning views of the sea and the nearby islands. Juan y Andrea is a restaurant that offers excellent service and quality.

Beso Beach: This is a restaurant located on the beachfront of Ses Illetes, near Juan y Andrea. It has a natural and bohemian decoration, with wooden tables and chairs, cushions, and candles. It offers Mediterranean cuisine with a fusion touch, such as tuna tartare, octopus salad, lamb chops, or cheesecake. It also has a bar with cocktails and music, and a shop with clothing and accessories. Beso Beach is a restaurant that offers a lively and fun atmosphere.

Can Carlos: This is a restaurant located in the center of Sant Francesc Xavier, the capital of the island. It has a cozy and elegant design, with white walls and furniture, wooden floors, and colorful paintings. It offers Italian cuisine with a creative twist, such as burrata salad, truffle pasta, sea bass fillet, or tiramisu. It also has a terrace with views of the town and the church. Can Carlos is a restaurant that offers high-quality service and food.

Es Molí de Sal: This is a restaurant located on the beachfront of Es Cavall d'en Borràs, near La Savina port. It is housed in an old salt mill that dates back to the 18th century, and has been renovated with respect for its history and architecture. It offers Mediterranean cuisine with local products, such as gazpacho, seafood rice, grilled fish, or almond cake. It also has a terrace with views of the sea and Es Vedrà island. Es Molí de Sal is a restaurant that offers a charming and romantic experience.

Can Dani: This is a restaurant located in the

countryside near Sant Ferran de Ses Roques, surrounded by gardens and olive trees. It is the first and only restaurant in Formentera that has a Michelin star, which it received in 2019. It offers a seasonal menu with innovative and exquisite dishes, such as scallop carpaccio, duck breast, or chocolate soufflé. It also has a wine cellar with more than 200 references. Can Dani is a restaurant that offers a luxurious and exclusive experience.

Chapter 5 • Ibiza Cuisine and Food Experiences

Introduction to Ibiza Cuisine

Ibiza is not only a paradise for party-goers, but also for food lovers. The island's cuisine is a delicious blend of Mediterranean and Balearic influences, with fresh seafood, meat, vegetables, fruits, herbs, and spices. Ibiza's cuisine reflects its history, culture, and geography, as well as its seasonal and local products. Below are some of the main features and dishes of Ibiza's cuisine:

Seafood: Being an island surrounded by the sea, Ibiza has a rich and varied seafood offer. You can find fish such as grouper, sea bass, red mullet, sardines, or mackerel, as well as shellfish such as prawns, mussels, clams, or lobster. Some of the most popular seafood dishes in Ibiza are bullit de peix (a fish stew with potatoes and aioli), guisat de peix (a fish casserole with almonds and saffron), borrida de ratjada (a ray stew with garlic and parsley), or frita de pulpo (fried octopus with potatoes and peppers).

Meat: Ibiza also has a strong meat tradition, especially pork and lamb. You can find local cold meats such as sobrasada (a cured sausage with paprika), butifarra (a fresh sausage with spices), or botifarró (a black pudding with rice). You can also find meat dishes such as sofrit pagès (a stew with chicken, lamb, potatoes, and sausages), arroz de matanza (a rice dish with pork and vegetables), or ensalada payesa (a salad with potatoes, peppers, onions, tomatoes, and cold meats).

Pastries: Ibiza has a sweet tooth and a variety of pastries to indulge in. You can find ensaimada (a spiral-shaped pastry with lard and sugar), flaó (a cheesecake with mint and aniseed), greixonera (a pudding with leftover ensaimada and eggs), orelletes (thin fried pastries with sugar and aniseed), or coca de albaricoque (a cake with apricot jam).

Drinks: Ibiza has some refreshing and aromatic drinks to quench your thirst or warm your soul. You can find horchata de chufa (a milky drink made from tiger nuts), café caleta (a coffee with brandy, lemon peel, cinnamon, and cloves), hierbas ibicencas (a herbal liqueur with aniseed), or frigola (liqueur distilled with wild thyme).

Regional Specialties

Ibiza is a melting pot of flavours, where you can taste the regional specialities of the island, as well as the influences of other Spanish and Mediterranean cuisines. Ibiza's regional specialities are based on the local products of the land and the sea, such as fish, seafood, meat, cheese, fruits, vegetables, herbs, and spices. Below are some of the regional specialities that you should try when visiting the island:

Sobrasada: This is a cured sausage made from pork, paprika, salt, and other spices. It has a soft texture and a reddish colour. It can be eaten raw, spread on bread, or cooked with other dishes. It is one of the most typical products of the Balearic Islands and has a protected geographical indication (PGI).

Botifarra: This is another type of sausage made from pork, blood, rice, and spices. It has a dark colour and a firm texture. It can be eaten grilled, fried, or boiled with vegetables. It is also a traditional product of the Balearic Islands and has a PGI.

Flaó: This is a cheesecake made from fresh cheese (usually sheep or goat cheese), eggs, sugar, mint, and aniseed. It has a round shape and a golden crust. It can be eaten as a dessert or as a snack. It is one of the oldest pastries on the island and also has a PGI.

Greixonera: This is a pudding made from leftover ensaimada (a spiral-shaped pastry with lard and sugar), eggs, milk, sugar, lemon peel, and cinnamon. It has a moist texture and a brown colour. It can be eaten hot or cold as a dessert or as a breakfast.

Orelletes: These are thin fried pastries made from flour, eggs, sugar, aniseed, and olive oil. They have an oval shape and are sprinkled with sugar. They can be eaten as a dessert or as a snack.

Sal de Ibiza: This is sea salt harvested from the natural salt flats of Ibiza. It has a white colour and a crunchy texture. It can be used to season any dish or to make salted products such as cheese or ham. It has a PGI.

Frita de pulpo: This is a dish made from octopus, potatoes, peppers, garlic, paprika, vinegar, and olive oil. It has a spicy flavour and a colourful appearance. It can be eaten as a main course or as a tapa (a small portion of food).

Ensalada payesa: This is a salad made from potatoes, peppers, onions, tomatoes, cold meats (such as sobrasada or botifarra), hard-boiled eggs, olives, and olive oil. It has a fresh flavour and a hearty texture. It can be eaten as a starter or as a light meal.

Arroz de matanza: This is a rice dish made from pork (usually from the slaughter of the pig), vegetables (such as artichokes or peas), saffron, and broth. It has a savoury flavour and a yellow colour. It can be eaten as a main course or as a side dish.

Cuinat: This is a vegetable stew made from cabbage, spinach, chard, chickpeas, garlic, mint, olive oil, and water. It has a green colour and a mild flavour. It can be eaten hot or cold as a main course or as an accompaniment.

Famous Ibiza Dishes

Below are some of the famous Ibiza dishes that you have to try when visiting the island:

Paella de Marisco: This is the classic Spanish rice dish with seafood, cooked with saffron, garlic, onion, tomato, and parsley. It is usually served in a large pan and shared among several people. You can find different types of seafood in the paella, such as prawns, mussels, clams, squid, or fish. It is a filling and flavorful dish that is perfect for a sunny day by the beach.

Flaó: This is a traditional Ibizan cheesecake made with

fresh cheese (usually sheep or goat cheese), eggs, sugar, mint, and aniseed. It has a round shape and a golden crust. It can be eaten as a dessert or as a snack. It is one of the oldest pastries on the island and has a protected geographical indication (PGI).

Greixonera: This is a pudding made from leftover ensaimada (a spiral-shaped pastry with lard and sugar), eggs, milk, sugar, lemon peel, and cinnamon. It has a moist texture and a brown colour. It can be eaten hot or cold as a dessert or as a breakfast.

Sofrit Pagés: This is a traditional Balearic stew made with various types of meat such as chicken, lamb, and the Ibizan sausages sobrassada and botifarra. There are also vegetables such as potatoes, peppers, and artichokes. It is seasoned with spices such as cinnamon, cloves, saffron, and paprika. It is a hearty and tasty dish that is usually served on special occasions.

Bullit de Peix: This is a delicious seafood stew made with boiled fish, potatoes, garlic, tomato, and saffron. It has a stock that is also used for its accompanying dish called arroz a banda (rice). It is one of the most popular fish dishes in Ibiza and one of the most traditional Ibiza dishes to try.

Tortilla: This is a potato and onion-based

omelette-type dish that you can find in every tapas bar and restaurant across Spain. It can be eaten hot or cold, plain or with cheese, ham, or peppers. It is a simple but satisfying dish that can be eaten as a starter or as a main course.

Ensalada Payesa: This is a salad made from roasted red and green peppers, boiled potatoes, tomatoes, onions, olives, boiled eggs, and cold meats such as sobrassada or botifarra. It has a fresh flavour and a hearty texture. It can be eaten as a starter or as a light meal.

Arroz de Matanza: This is a rice dish made from pork (usually from the slaughter of the pig), vegetables such as artichokes or peas, saffron, and broth. It has a savoury flavour and a yellow colour. It can be eaten as a main course or as a side dish.

Cuinat: This is a vegetable stew made from cabbage, spinach, chard, chickpeas, garlic, mint, olive oil, and water. It has a green colour and a mild flavour. It can be eaten hot or cold as a main course or as an accompaniment.

Zarzuela de Mariscos: This is another seafood stew made with shellfish such as mussels, crabs, scallops, and prawns, with squid and various types of fish. It is cooked in a saffron-flavoured stock, usually mixed with lemon juice and bay leaf. It is similar to bullit de peix, but more elaborate and rich.

Wine and Food Pairing

Ibiza is a paradise for wine lovers, as the island produces some of the finest wines in the Mediterranean, with a variety of grapes, styles, and flavours. Below are some of the wine and food pairing suggestions that you can try when visiting Ibiza:

White wine: White wine is ideal for seafood dishes, as it enhances the freshness and delicacy of the fish and shellfish. You can pair a crisp and fruity white wine, such as a Malvasia or a Chardonnay, with dishes such as paella de marisco, bullit de peix, zarzuela de mariscos, or frita de pulpo. You can also pair a dry and aromatic white wine, such as a Sauvignon Blanc or a Gewürztraminer, with dishes such as ensalada payesa, flaó, or greixonera.

Rosé wine: Rosé wine is perfect for meat dishes, as it balances the richness and spiciness of the pork and lamb. You can pair a light and refreshing rosé wine, such as a Merlot or a Pinot Noir, with dishes such as sofrit pagés, arroz de matanza, or botifarra sausages. You can also pair a medium-bodied and fruity rosé wine, such as a Syrah or a Grenache, with dishes such as tortilla, cuinat, or bread with tomato.

Red wine: Red wine is great for cheese dishes, as it complements the creaminess and intensity of the sheep and goat cheese. You can pair a full-bodied and complex red wine, such as a Cabernet Sauvignon or a Tempranillo, with dishes such as sobrassada, sal de Ibiza cheese, or bread with alioli. You can also pair a smooth and elegant red wine, such as a Monastrell or a Pinotage, with dishes such as molleja (gizzard), orelletes, or bread with tomato.

Culinary Experiences and Cooking Classes

Ibiza is a culinary destination with a variety of experiences and classes for food lovers who want to learn more about the island's gastronomy, culture, and history. Below are some of the culinary experiences and cooking classes that you can try when visiting Ibiza:

Cook with Chef Ibiza: This is a personalized in-villa cooking experience that allows you to learn from a local chef how to prepare some of the most iconic dishes of Ibiza, such as paella, tapas, bullit de peix, or flaó. You can also choose to forage or visit a farm to source some of the fresh ingredients for your meal. You will enjoy a hands-on cooking session, followed by a delicious feast with your friends or family.

Instituto de Idiomas Ibiza: This is a language school that also offers cooking classes in Spanish or English. You can learn how to make some of the typical Spanish and Ibizan dishes, such as tortilla, gazpacho, croquetas, or ensalada payesa. You will also learn about the history and culture of the island and its cuisine, as well as practice your language skills with other students and teachers.

Camino Verde Ibiza: This is an eco-friendly tour company that offers hiking and camping tours with a culinary twist. You can explore the natural beauty of the island while learning about its flora and fauna, as well as its culinary traditions. You will also enjoy a picnic or a barbecue with local products, such as cheese, bread, wine, or sobrassada.

Southside Bars: This is a cocktail bar that also offers cocktail-making classes. You can learn how to mix and shake some of the classic and signature cocktails of

Ibiza, such as sangria, mojito, caipirinha, or hierbas ibicencas. You will also learn about the history and culture of the island and its drinks, as well as have fun with your friends or colleagues.

Moos Salad Delivery: This is a healthy food delivery service that also offers salad-making classes. You can learn how to create your salads with fresh and organic ingredients, such as lettuce, tomatoes, avocado, nuts, seeds, or dressing. You will also learn about the nutritional benefits of each ingredient, as well as how to customize your salads according to your preferences.

Chapter 6 • Outdoor Activities and Nature

Clubbing in Ibiza

Ibiza is the world's clubbing capital, where you can experience some of the best parties, DJs, and venues on the planet. Ibiza's clubs are open from May to October, with the peak season being July and August. Below are some of the main things you need to know about clubbing in Ibiza:

Where to go: Ibiza's clubs are scattered across the island, but there are two main areas for clubbing: Playa d'en Bossa and San Antonio. Playa d'en Bossa is on the east coast of the island, and it's home to some of the biggest and most famous clubs, such as Hï Ibiza, Ushuaïa, and Octan. San Antonio is on the west coast of the island, and it's known for its sunset cafes, bars, and clubs, such as Ibiza Rocks, O Beach Ibiza, Es Paradis, and Eden. There are also other clubs around the island, such as Pacha in Ibiza Town, Amnesia and Privilege in San Rafael, DC-10 in Sant Josep de sa Talaia, and Lío in Talamanca.

When to go: Ibiza's clubs usually open around midnight and close around 6 or 7 am. However, some clubs have daytime or evening parties as well, such as Ushuaïa, Destino Pacha, or Hard Rock Hotel Ibiza. The best time to go to a club depends on your preference and budget. If you want to avoid crowds and save some money, you can go early in the season (May or June) or late in the season (September or October). If you want to experience the peak of the party scene and see the biggest DJs and acts, you can go in July or August. However, be prepared to pay more for tickets and drinks, and to queue longer at the entrance.

How to get tickets: There are different ways to get tickets for clubs in Ibiza. You can buy them online in advance from official websites or authorized sellers. This can save you time and money, as you can avoid queues and get discounts or special offers. You can also buy them at bars and stores around the island. This can be convenient if you're not sure which club or party you want to go to. You can also get wristbands from promoters or dancers who go around the beaches or streets offering deals or discounts for certain parties. However, be careful not to buy fake or overpriced tickets from unauthorized sellers.

What to wear: Ibiza's clubs have a relaxed and informal dress code, so you can wear whatever you like. However, some tips can help you fit in and have a comfortable night out. For example, you can wear light and breathable fabrics that can keep you cool in the hot weather. You can also wear comfortable shoes that can protect your feet from stepping on glass or getting stepped on by others. You can also accessorize your outfit with sunglasses, hats, jewellery, or glow sticks that can add some fun and flair to your look.

What to expect: Ibiza's clubs offer an unforgettable experience that can blow your mind with their music, atmosphere, and visuals. You can expect to hear some of the best DJs and live acts in the world playing a variety of genres and styles. You can also expect to see some of the most impressive lighting and sound systems that can create a stunning sensory show. You can also expect to meet some of the most friendly people from all over the world who share your passion for music and partying.

Hiking and Trekking in Ibiza

Ibiza is not only a party island, but also a natural paradise that offers a variety of hiking and trekking opportunities for outdoor lovers. Ibiza has over 100 hiking trails that range from easy to challenging, from short to long, and from coastal to inland. Below are some of the main things you need to know about hiking and trekking in Ibiza:

Where to go: Ibiza's trails cover different areas of the island, but some regions are especially popular for hiking and trekking. For example, the north of the island is known for its rugged and wild scenery, with cliffs, coves, forests, and hills. Some of the best trails in this area are Puig des Savinar, Far des Moscarter, and Ses Balandres. The south of the island is known for its scenic and cultural attractions, with beaches, salt flats, towers, and caves. Some of the best trails in this area are Torre d'en Rovira, Es Cubells, and Sa Pedrera. The east of the island is known for its green and peaceful landscape, with valleys, farms, orchards, and villages. Some of the best trails in this area are Puig de ses Torretes, Camí de s'Argentera, or Cala de s'Aigua Dolça. The west of the island is known for its spectacular and diverse views, with islands, mountains, vineyards, and sunsets. Some of the best trails in this area are Torre des Savinar, Sa Talaia, and Cala Bassa.

When to go: Ibiza's climate is mild and sunny all year

round, but some seasons are more suitable for hiking and trekking than others. The best time to go is spring (March to May) or autumn (September to November), when the weather is pleasant and not too hot or cold, nature is colourful and fragrant, and the trails are not too crowded or noisy. The summer (June to August) can be too hot and dry for hiking and trekking, especially during midday or afternoon. However, you can still enjoy some trails that are near the sea or have shade along the way. The winter (December to February) can be too cold and wet for hiking and trekking, especially in the higher areas or during rainy days. However, you can still enjoy some trails that are lower or have sunny spots along the way.

How to prepare: Ibiza's trails are well-marked and maintained, but some tips can help you prepare for a safe and enjoyable hike or trek. For example, you should wear comfortable and appropriate clothing and footwear that can protect you from the sun, heat, cold, or rain. You should also bring enough water and snacks to keep you hydrated and energized during your hike or trek. You should also bring a map or a GPS device to help you navigate your trail and avoid getting lost. You should also inform someone about your route and expected return time before you start your hike or trek. You should also respect the nature and culture of the island by not littering, making noise, or trespassing on private property.

What to expect: Ibiza's trails offer an amazing experience that can enrich your mind, body, and soul with their beauty, diversity, and history. You can expect to see some of the most breathtaking views of the sea, the islands, the mountains, and the sky. You can also expect to discover some of the most fascinating sites of the island's heritage, such as towers, lighthouses, caves, and churches. You can also expect to meet some of the most friendly and welcoming people in the island's community, such as farmers, shepherds, or locals.

Cycling in Ibiza

Ibiza is a cycling paradise that offers a variety of routes and experiences for bike lovers of all levels and styles. Ibiza has over 100 cycling routes that range from easy to expert, from short to long, and from road to gravel. Below are some of the main things you need to know about cycling in Ibiza:

Where to go: Ibiza's routes cover different areas of the island, but some regions are especially popular for cycling. For example, the south of the island is known for its flat and smooth roads, with salt flats, beaches, towers, and caves. Some of the best routes in this area are Torre de Ses Portes, Es Cubells, and Sa Pedrera. The north of the island is known for its hilly and wild terrain, with cliffs, coves, forests, and farms. Some of the best routes in this area are Far des Moscarter, Puig des Savinar, or Ses Balandres. The east of the island is known for its green and peaceful landscape, with valleys, orchards, villages, and churches. Some of the best routes in this area are Puig de ses Torretes, Camí de s'Argentera, or Cala de s'Aigua Dolça. The west of the island is known for its spectacular and diverse views, with islands, mountains, vineyards, and sunsets. Some of the best routes in this area are Torre d'en Rovira, Sa Talaia, or Cala Bassa.

When to go: Ibiza's climate is mild and sunny all year round, but some seasons are more suitable for cycling than others. The best time to go is spring (March to May) or autumn (September to November), when the weather is pleasant and not too hot or cold, nature is crisp and fragrant, and the roads are not too crowded or noisy. The summer (June to August) can be too hot and dry for cycling, especially during midday or afternoon. However, you can still enjoy some routes that are near the sea or have shade along the way. The winter (December to February) can be too cold and wet for cycling, especially in the higher areas or during rainy days. However, you can still enjoy some routes that are lower or have sunny spots along the way.

How to prepare: Ibiza's routes are well-marked and maintained, but some tips can help you prepare for a safe and enjoyable ride. For example, you should wear comfortable and appropriate clothing and footwear that can protect you from the sun, heat, cold, or rain. You should also bring enough water and snacks to keep you hydrated and energized during your ride. You should also bring a map or a GPS device to help you navigate your route and avoid getting lost. You should also inform someone about your route and expected return time before you start your ride. You should also respect the nature and culture of the island by not littering, making noise, or trespassing on private property.

What to expect: Ibiza's routes has amazing experiences that can enrich your mind, body, and soul with their beauty and history. You can expect to see some of the most breathtaking views of the sea, the islands, the mountains, and the sky. You can also expect to meet some of the most friendly and welcoming people in the island's community, such as farmers, shepherds, or locals.

Watersports in Ibiza

Ibiza is a watersports paradise that offers a variety of activities and experiences for water lovers of all levels and styles. Ibiza has over 200 beaches and coves that provide the perfect setting for watersports, as well as many centres and operators that offer equipment hire and lessons. Below are some of the main things you need to know about watersports in Ibiza:

What to do: Ibiza's watersports cover different types of activities, but some are especially popular and fun. For example, scuba diving and snorkelling are great ways to explore the underwater world of Ibiza, with its rich marine life, caves, wrecks, and reefs. Some of the best spots for diving and snorkelling are Cala d'Hort, Es Vedrà, Cala Llonga, or Cala Comte. Kayaking and paddle boarding are great ways to enjoy the scenic views of the coast, with its cliffs, coves, islands, and sunsets. Some of the best spots for kayaking and paddle boarding are

Portinatx, Cala Bassa, Cala Tarida, and Es Cubells. Jet skiing and speed boating are great ways to experience the adrenaline and excitement of the sea, with its speed, power, and spray. Some of the best spots for jet skiing and speed boating are Playa d'en Bossa, San Antonio Bay, Santa Eulalia, and Formentera. Parasailing and flyboarding are great ways to experience the thrill and freedom of the air, with its height, wind, and views. Some of the best spots for parasailing and flyboarding are San Antonio Bay, Playa d'en Bossa, Cala Jondal, and Talamanca.

When to go: Ibiza's climate is mild and sunny all year round, but some seasons are more suitable for watersports than others. The best time to go is summer (June to September) when the water temperature is warm and pleasant, the wind is light and steady, and the sea conditions are calm and clear. The spring (March to May) and autumn (October to November) can also be good times to go when the water temperature is still comfortable, the wind is moderate and variable, and the sea conditions are still good. The winter (December to February) can be too cold and wet for watersports, especially in the north of the island or during stormy days. However, you can still find some activities that are available in the south of the island or on sunny days.

How to prepare: Ibiza's watersports are safe and accessible for everyone, but some tips can help you prepare for a fun experience. For example, you should wear comfortable and appropriate clothing and footwear that can protect you from the sun, salt water, or jellyfish. You should also bring enough water and sunscreen to keep you hydrated and protected during your activity. You should also bring a valid ID card or passport to show at the centre or operator before your activity. You should also follow the instructions and rules of your guide or instructor during your activity. You should also respect the nature and culture of the island by not littering, making noise, or disturbing other people or animals.

What to expect: Ibiza's watersports offer an amazing experience that can enrich your mind, body, and soul with their beauty and fun. You can expect to see some of the most stunning views of the sea, the islands, the sky, and the coast. You can also expect to discover some of the most amazing sites of the island's nature, such as caves, wrecks, reefs, and dolphins. You can also expect to feel some of the most exhilarating sensations of the water, such as speed, power, height, or weightlessness.

Skiing in Ibiza

Ibiza is not a typical skiing destination, but it does offer some unique and fun opportunities for skiing enthusiasts who want to try something different and adventurous. Below are some of the main things you need to know about skiing in Ibiza:

What to do: Ibiza's skiing activities cover different types of sports, but some are especially popular and fun. For example, water skiing and jet skiing are great ways to enjoy the speed and excitement of skiing on the sea, with its waves, spray, and views. Some of the best spots for water skiing and jet skiing are Playa d'en Bossa, San Antonio Bay, Cala Bassa, and Formentera. Snow skiing and snowboarding are great ways to enjoy the thrill and challenge of skiing on snow, with its slopes, jumps, and tricks. Some of the best spots for snow skiing and snowboarding are Andorra, Sierra Nevada, and the Pyrenees, which are accessible by ferry or plane from Ibiza. Sand skiing and sandboarding are great ways to enjoy the fun and novelty of skiing on sand, with its dunes, curves, and slides. Some of the best spots for sand skiing and sandboarding are Las Salinas, Es Cavallet, and Ses Salines Natural Park.

When to go: Ibiza's climate is mild and sunny all year round, but some seasons are more suitable for skiing than others. The best time to go is summer (June to September) when the water temperature is warm and pleasant, the wind is light and steady, and the sea conditions are calm and clear for water skiing and jet skiing. The spring (March to May) and autumn (October to November) can also be good times to go when the water temperature is still comfortable, the wind is moderate and variable, and the sea conditions are still good for water skiing and jet skiing. The winter (December to February) can be too cold and wet for water skiing and jet skiing, especially in the north of the island or during stormy days. However, you can still find some activities that are available in the south of the island or during sunny days for water skiing and jet skiing. Winter is also the best time to go for snow skiing and snowboarding when the snow conditions are optimal and fresh in Andorra, Sierra Nevada, or the Pyrenees.

How to prepare: Ibiza's skiing activities are safe and accessible for everyone, but some tips can help you prepare for a fun experience. For example, you should wear comfortable and appropriate clothing and footwear that can protect you from the sun, salt water, or jellyfish for water skiing and jet skiing. You should also bring enough water and sunscreen to keep you hydrated and protected during your activity. You should also bring a valid ID card or passport to show at the centre or operator before your activity. You should also follow the instructions and rules of your guide or instructor during your activity. You should also respect the nature and culture of the island by not littering, making noise, or disturbing other people or animals. For snow skiing and snowboarding, you should wear warm and waterproof clothing and footwear that can protect you from the cold, snow, or ice. For sand skiing and sandboarding, you should wear light and breathable clothing and footwear that can protect you from the sun, sand, or wind. You should also bring enough water and sunscreen to keep you hydrated and protected during your activity. You should also bring a hat, sunglasses, and scarf to shield your face and head from the sun and sand.

What to expect: Ibiza's skiing activities offer an amazing experience that can enrich your mind, body, and soul with their beauty, diversity, and fun. You can expect to see some of the most stunning views of the sea, the islands, the sky, and the coast for water skiing and jet skiing. You can also expect to discover some of the most amazing sites of the island's nature, such as caves, wrecks, reefs, or dolphins for water skiing and jet skiing. You can also expect to feel some of the most exhilarating sensations of the water, such as speed, power, height, or weightlessness for water skiing and jet skiing. You can expect to see some of the most breathtaking views of the snow, the mountains, the forests, and the villages for snow skiing and snowboarding. You can also expect to discover some of the most fascinating sites of the destination's heritage, such as churches, castles, monuments, or museums for snow skiing and snowboarding. You can also expect to feel some of the most thrilling sensations of the snow, such as slope, jump, trick, or slide for snow skiing and snowboarding. You can expect to see some of the most beautiful views of the sand, the dunes, the cacti, and the birds for sand skiing and sandboarding. You can also expect to discover some of the most interesting sites of the island's nature, such as salt flats, lagoons, flamingos, or turtles for sand skiing and sandboarding. You can also expect to feel some of the most fun sensations of the sand, such as curve, spin, flip, or glide for sand skiing and sandboarding.

Exploring National Parks

Ibiza is a natural paradise that offers a variety of natural parks and reserves for nature lovers of all levels and styles. Ibiza has two main natural parks and several natural reserves that protect and showcase the island's ecological and cultural diversity. Below are some of the main things you need to know about exploring national parks in Ibiza:

What to see: Ibiza's natural parks and reserves cover different types of landscapes, but some are especially remarkable and beautiful. For example, Ses Salines Natural Park is a wetland area situated between the south of Ibiza and the north of Formentera, covering an area of 1,786 hectares on land and 13,612 hectares offshore. It features salt lakes, beaches, dunes, forests, cliffs, and islands, as well as a variety of flora and fauna, such as flamingos, herons, seagulls, lizards, orchids, junipers, and pines. It also has historical and cultural sites, such as salt pans, towers, churches, and Phoenician settlements. Es Vedrà, Es Vedranell, and the Western Islets Natural Reserve is a marine and terrestrial area situated to the southwest of Ibiza, covering an area of 2,351 hectares on land and 13,617 hectares offshore. It features rocky islands, a marine environment, hills, streams, beaches, and caves, as well as a variety of flora and fauna, such as dolphins, turtles, fish, birds, lizards, cacti, and flowers. It also has historical and cultural sites, such as lighthouses, caves, and legends.

When to go: Ibiza's climate is mild and sunny all year round, but some seasons are more suitable for exploring national parks than others. The best time to go is spring (March to May) or autumn (September to November), when the weather is pleasant and not too hot or cold, nature is colourful and fragrant, and the parks are not too crowded or noisy. The summer (June to August) can be too hot and dry for exploring national parks, especially during midday or afternoon. However, you can still enjoy some parks that are near the sea or have shade along the way. The winter (December to February) can be too cold and wet for exploring national parks, especially in the higher areas or during rainy days. However, you can still enjoy some parks that are lower or have sunny spots along the way.

How to get there: Ibiza's natural parks and reserves

are accessible by different means of transport, but some tips can help you get there in a convenient and eco-friendly way. For example, you can take a bus or a taxi to the main entrances or visitor centres of the parks or reserves, where you can get information, maps, and guides. You can also take a ferry or a boat to some of the islands or coves that are part of the parks or reserves, where you can enjoy the views, the water, and the wildlife. You can also rent a bike or a scooter to explore some of the trails or roads that go through or near the parks or reserves, where you can enjoy the scenery, the exercise, and the freedom. You can also walk or hike to some of the paths or routes that go through or around the parks or reserves, where you can enjoy nature, adventure, and peace.

What to do: Ibiza's natural parks and reserves offer a variety of activities and experiences for nature lovers of all levels and styles. For example, you can admire the stunning scenery of the sea, the islands, the mountains, and the sky. You can observe the rich wildlife of flamingos, dolphins, turtles, lizards, and birds. You can learn about the historical heritage of salt pans, towers, churches, and Phoenician settlements. You can also do some sports or hobbies that are compatible with nature conservation, such as snorkelling, diving, kayaking, fishing, birdwatch, cycling, camping, and picnicking.

Beaches and Coastal Escapes

Ibiza is a beach lover's paradise that offers a variety of beaches and coastal escapes for all tastes and moods. Ibiza has over 200 beaches and coves that range from long and wide to small and secluded, from lively and popular to quiet and remote, from white and smooth to rocky and rugged. Below are some of the main things you need to know about beaches and coastal escapes in Ibiza:

What to see: Ibiza's beaches and coastal escapes cover different types of landscapes, but some are especially remarkable and beautiful. For example, Cala Comte is a stunning beach with turquoise water, white sand, and views of the islands of Es Vedrà and Es Vedranell. It is one of the best places to watch the sunset in Ibiza, with several bars and restaurants along the shore. Cala Mastella is a tranquil cove with green water, silver sand, and pine trees. It is also the setting for one of Ibiza's most famous beach restaurants, El Bigotes, where you can enjoy a delicious fish stew or grilled fish. Cala

Saladeta is a blissful beach with crystal water, golden sand, and rocky cliffs. It is accessed by a short walk from the nearby Cala Salada, and it is one of the most pristine and peaceful beaches in Ibiza. Cala Tarida is a popular beach with blue water, fine sand, and a variety of services and facilities. It is also one of the best beaches for water sports in Ibiza, with jet skis, kayaks, paddle boards, and more available for rent.

When to go: Ibiza's climate is mild and sunny all year round, but some seasons are more suitable for beaches and coastal escapes than others. The best time to go is summer (June to September) when the water temperature is warm and pleasant, the wind is light and steady, and the sea conditions are calm and clear. The spring (March to May) and autumn (October to November) can also be good times to go when the water temperature is still comfortable, the wind is moderate and variable, and the sea conditions are still good. The winter (December to February) can be too cold and wet for beaches and coastal escapes, especially in the north of the island or during stormy days. However, you can still find some beaches that are open and sunny in the south of the island or during clear days.

How to get there: Ibiza's beaches and coastal escapes

are accessible by different means of transport, but some tips can help you get there in a convenient and eco-friendly way. For example, you can take a bus or a taxi to the main entrances or parking areas of the beaches or coves, where you can get information, maps, and guides. You can also take a ferry or a boat to some of the islands or coves that are not reachable by land, where you can enjoy the views, the water, and the wildlife. You can also rent a bike or a scooter to explore some of the trails or roads that go along or near the coast, where you can enjoy the scenery, the exercise, and the freedom. You can also walk or hike to some of the paths or routes that go to or around the beaches or coves, where you can enjoy nature, advice, and peace.

What to do: Ibiza's beaches and coastal escapes offer a variety of activities and experiences for beach lovers of all levels and styles. For example, you can relax on the soft sand, swim in the clear water, sunbathe under the sun, or read under an umbrella. You can party with the crowds, dance to the music, drink at the bars, or eat at the restaurants. You can explore the hidden coves, snorkel in the reefs, dive in the caves, or kayak in the waves. You can also do some sports or hobbies that are compatible with beach conservation, such as surfing, windsurfing, kite surfing, sailing, fishing, birdwatpicnic nic, and camping.

Chapter 7 • Shopping in Ibiza

Fashion and Luxury Shopping

Ibiza is not only a paradise for party-goers, but also for shoppers who love fashion and luxury. The island offers a variety of stylish boutiques, concept stores, markets and galleries where you can find everything from high-end designer labels to unique local creations. Below are some of the best places to shop in Ibiza.

De Mil Amores

If you're looking for a one-stop shop for all your fashion needs, head to De Mil Amores in Ibiza Town. This boutique has been on the scene for over 20 years and offers a curated selection of clothing, shoes, bags, jewellery and sunglasses from some of the most popular brands in the world. You can find Balmain, Dsquared2, Moschino, Versace, Valentino and many more. De Mil Amores also has its line of exclusive designs that reflect the Ibiza style: colourful, fun and glamorous. You'll find something to love here.

IBIZA REPUBLIC

If you want to show your love for Ibiza, check out IBIZA REPUBLIC in Ibiza Town. This store specializes in t-shirts, sweatshirts, hoodies, caps and bags with original designs inspired by the island's culture, history and lifestyle. You can find slogans like "Ibiza is my religion", "Ibiza is not Spain" or "Ibiza is always a good idea". You can also customize your t-shirt with your name, logo or message. IBIZA REPUBLIC is the perfect place to get a souvenir or a gift for your friends and family. The IBIZA REPUBLIC is open every day from 11:00 to 13:30 and from 18:00 to 22:00.

Treasure Chest at Experimental Beach Ibiza

What better way to shop than midway through a cocktail at Experimental Beach Club? The on-site boutique, which originally started as a temporary project called The Space, stocks unique one-offs and is a real champion for local Ibizan designers. Here you can find scarves by Beshlie McKelvie, stunning embellished evening wear by Kurru Kurru and pretty pieces from Zara Simon's latest jewellery collection, as well as a good stock of swimwear for the guys. Tortu Artwear is the standout brand here however – a range of locally handmade bikinis, no two of which are alike so you're guaranteed to never bump into your swimsuit twin on the beach. Treasure Chest at Experimental Beach Ibiza is open every day from 10:00 to 02:00.

Beatrice San Francisco

Beatrice San Francisco is an essential pit stop for everything you need to achieve that Ibiza boho-chic look. The shop in Vara de Rey hosts a collection of some of the most famous brands to come from the island itself such as World Family, Apachestyle, Don Quixote, Moksha, Anne Von Kattle and Beija Flor. The star of the show however is Beatrice San Francisco herself – a Dutch designer who has been living in Ibiza since she was six years old and whose creations have been worn by celebrities like Shakira, Paris Hilton and Naomi Campbell. Her signature style is based on natural fabrics like cotton and bamboo that are dyed in earthy tones and feature crochet details, fringes and asymmetrical cuts. Her pieces are versatile, comfortable and flattering for any body type. Beatrice San Francisco is open every day from 10:30 to 22:30.

Local Markets and Souvenirs

Ibiza offers a variety of markets where you can find everything from handicrafts, organic food, second-hand items, and of course, the famous hippie style that characterizes Ibiza. Below are some of the best places to shop in Ibiza.

Las Dalias

Las Dalias is one of the most iconic and legendary markets in Ibiza. It started in 1954 as a roadside bar and has evolved into a cultural and artistic hub that attracts thousands of visitors every week. On Saturdays, you can find over 200 stalls in the gardens, selling almost everything: fabrics, handmade clothes, Ibiza's famous AdLib fashions, costume jewellery, artisanal goods, decoration, hammocks... You can also enjoy live music, concerts and DJ sessions in the evening and at night. On Mondays and Tuesdays from June to September and on Sundays in July and August, there is a night market with a more intimate and magical atmosphere. There are also special markets at Easter and Christmas. Las Dalias is open every day from 11:00 to 01:00.

Mercadillo Sant Jordi

Mercadillo Sant Jordi is a second-hand market that is held on Saturday mornings in the former horse-racing track of Sant Jordi, in the south of the island. This is the favourite among the island's residents, who come here to look for bargains or sell off their unwanted items. You can find all kinds of second-hand items here, such as records, books, furniture, clothing, luggage, etc. You can also have a snack at the bar and enjoy the midday percussion sessions led by musicians in the bleachers. This is a great place to mingle with the locals and discover the authentic side of Ibiza. Mercadillo Sant Jordi is open every Saturday from 08:00 to 15:00.

Mercat Vell

Mercat Vell is a historic market that dates back to the 19th century. It is located in the heart of Ibiza Town, next to the Portal de Ses Taules entrance to Dalt Vila (the old town). Here you can find fresh fruits and vegetables from local farmers, as well as flowers, herbs and spices. The market is open every day from morning until evening, except on Sundays. You can also enjoy the lively atmosphere of the Plaza de la Constitución, where there are many cafes and restaurants to relax and watch the world go by. Mercat Vell is open every day except Sunday from 07:00 to 14:00.

Santa Eulalia Market

Santa Eulalia Market is a market that takes place every Wednesday on the iconic Paseo de S'Alamera boulevard in Santa Eulalia del Río, on the east coast of Ibiza. Here you can find over 100 stalls selling handicrafts, jewellery, clothing, accessories, leather goods and more. You can also enjoy live music and performances by local artists. The market is open from April to October from 10:00 to 14:00. You can also visit the nearby Marina Market on Saturdays from May to October from 18:00 to midnight. Santa Eulalia Market is open every Wednesday from April to October from 10:00 to 14:00.

Artisan Crafts and Workshops

Ibiza is also for craft lovers who want to learn new skills, express their creativity and make their souvenirs. The island offers a variety of workshops where you can learn from local artisans and experts in different fields, such as embroidery, macramé, weaving, fabric flowers, painting, cardboard crafts, pressed flower crafts, ceramics and upcycling. Below are some of the best places to join a craft workshop in Ibiza.

La Luna Gallery

La Luna Gallery is a curated online and physical space created to share the healing power of expressive arts. This project is here to support creativity and connection, offering a variety of conscious creative workshops, expressive arts inspiration and creative retreats online and on the island of Ibiza. You can dive into the creative spirit through guided exploration most intimately and authentically, discovering a carefully made selection of treasured experiences and wisdom through the arts. Some of the workshops you can join are fabric flower making, natural dyeing, macramé wall hanging, weaving mandalas, embroidery hoop art and more. La Luna Gallery is located in Santa Eulalia del Río.

Le Petit Atelier n°74

Le Petit Atelier n°74 is a cosy and charming space where you can discover the creative worlds of embroidery, macramé, weaving, fabric flowers, painting, cardboard crafts, pressed flower crafts and more. The workshops are designed to awaken your innate talents and invite you to feel the joy that we find in creating with our hands. You can also enjoy delicious tea or coffee while you craft. The workshops are suitable for all levels and ages, and you can book them online or by phone. Le Petit Atelier n°74 is located in Santa Gertrudis de Fruitera.

Get Your Guide

Get Your Guide is an online platform where you can find and book a variety of activities and experiences in Ibiza and around the world. You can choose from different categories, such as arts and crafts workshops, tours, summer activities, outdoor activities and more. You can also read reviews from other travellers, compare prices and availability, and enjoy free cancellation up to 24 hours before your activity starts. Some of the craft workshops you can join in Ibizaarer: a walking tour of Dalt Vila with an art workshop, a guided tour of Dalt Vila with a handcraft workshop, a pottery workshop with local artists and more. Get Your Guide is available online.

Antique and Vintage Shopping

Ibiza is also for antique and vintage lovers who want to find unique and original items from different eras and cultures. The island offers a variety of shops and markets where you can find everything from clothing, accessories, furniture, ceramics, jewellery and more. Below are some of the best places to shop for antiques and vintage in Ibiza.

Bome Ibiza

Bome Ibiza is a speciality and gift shop that also features an art gallery. It is located in the old town of Ibiza, near the cathedral. Here you can find a selection of antique and vintage items, such as furniture, lamps, mirrors, paintings, sculptures and more. You can also admire the works of local and international artists, such as paintings, photographs, collages and installations. Bome Ibiza is a place where art and history meet, offering a unique shopping experience. Bome Ibiza is open every day from 10:00 to 22:00.

Holala Ibiza

Holala Ibiza is one of the most iconic and legendary vintage shops in Ibiza. It has been running since 1981 and has stores in Paris, LA, Saint Tropez and Barcelona. It is located in the centre of Ibiza Town, near the port. Here you can find vintage clothing carefully handpicked from every corner of the world. You can find brands such as Balmain, Dsquared2, Moschino, Versace, Valentino and many more. You can also find accessories, shoes, bags, jewellery and sunglasses. Holala Ibiza has been featured in Vogue UK and Elle Spain and has attracted celebrities such as Kate Moss and Dolce & Gabbana. Holala Ibiza is open every day from 11:00 to 01:00.

Vincente Ganesha

Vincente Ganesha is the oldest fashion store in Ibiza and a must-visit for fashion fans. It is part boutique, part costume cupboard, filled with everything from antique matador outfits to vintage Dior. You can rummage through rails of pieces from the '60s, '70s and '80s. You can also find exotic finds from the founder's travels around the world. The entrance is hidden by endless rails of clothes and the indoor vintage section is VIP only, meaning you get a personal shopping experience. Vincente Ganesha is open every day from 10:00 to 22:00.

Santa Eulalia Market

Santa Eulalia Market is a market that takes place every Wednesday on the iconic Paseo de S'Alamera boulevard in Santa Eulalia del Río, on the east coast of Ibiza. Here you can find over 100 stalls selling handicrafts, jewellery, clothing, accessories, leather goods and more. You can also find some antique and vintage items, such as books, records, posters, cameras and more. You can also enjoy live music and performances by local artists. Santa Eulalia Market is open every Wednesday from April to October from 10:00 to 14:00.

Wellness: Spas, Retreats, and Yoga

Ibiza is also for wellness seekers who want to relax, rejuvenate and reconnect with themselves. The island offers a variety of spas, yoga studios and retreats where you can enjoy treatments, therapies, classes and workshops that cater to your physical, mental and emotional needs. Below are some of the best places to experience wellness in Ibiza.

Six Senses Ibiza

Six Senses Ibiza is a luxury resort that combines wellness, sustainability and music in a stunning location on the north coast of Ibiza. Here you can escape the stresses of daily life and let the mind and body wind down with expert-led wellness retreats that are designed to provide much-needed space to reconnect with your inner peace and thrive when you're back in the outer world. You can choose from different themes, such as immunity, longevity, yoga and self-discovery, and immerse yourself in guided activities, therapies and workshops. You can also enjoy the state-of-the-art spa, the rooftop yoga pavilion, the organic farm and the recording studio. Six Senses Ibiza is open all year round.

Atzaro Agroturismo Hotel

Atzaro Agroturismo Hotel is a rustic-chic country estate that dates back 300 years ago. It is located in the heart of Ibiza, surrounded by perfumed gardens and dreamy courtyards. Here you can experience the authentic essence of Ibiza with a range of wellness offerings that are rooted in nature. You can join daily yoga classes in a stylish pavilion or on a Jacuzzi deck among the orange trees, meditate by an outdoor fire-pit lounge, enjoy treatments in a Balinese-inspired spa or relax by a 43-meter freshwater swimming pool. You can also join special events such as full moon yoga, sound healing and wellness festivals. Atzaro Agroturismo Hotel is open all year round.

7Pines Resort

7Pines Resort is a whitewashed, all-suite resort that is located in a pine forest, with grandstand sea views over Es Vedra, an islet off the southwest coast of Ibiza reputed to have mystical healing powers. Here you can take full advantage of that screensaver setting by practising yoga on the cliff edge, meditating under the full moon or enjoying treatments in the Pure Seven spa that uses natural and organic products. You can also join wellness retreats that combine yoga, meditation, nutrition and coaching to help you achieve your goals and transform your life. 7Pines Resort is open from April to October.

Chapter 8 • Practical Information

Health and Safety Tips

Ibiza is a beautiful and fun destination, but it also has some health and safety risks that you should be aware of and prepared for. Below are some tips to help you enjoy your trip without any unwanted surprises.

Sunburn

The sun in Ibiza can be very strong, especially in the summer months. To avoid painful and damaging sunburn, you should apply sunblock with a high SPF to all exposed areas of your body, especially the tops of your feet, backs of calves, thighs, buttocks, breasts, lips, nose, forehead and shoulders. You should reapply sunblock every couple of hours and especially after swimming. No sun cream is 100% waterproof. You should also wear a hat, sunglasses and cover-up clothing when possible. If you do get sunburnt, a good tip is to apply vinegar (the colder the better) to the affected area and this will soothe it and help prevent peeling. Aloe vera gel is also a great aid in soothing sunburnt skin and is available all over the island.

Food and water

Drinking iced beverages in the blazing Ibiza sun can cause severe temperature clashes in your system which can lead to upset stomachs, sore throats and dizziness. It is best to stick to body-temperature drinks in the sun and leave the iced drinks until you are sitting cooler in the shade, or later in the evening when the sun is going down. Although the local water is generally safe to drink in Ibiza, it is often not drinkable, so we recommend buying bottled water. You will find it cheaper overall to buy the big 5-litre or 8-litre bottles. You should also be careful with street food and avoid eating anything that looks undercooked or unhygienic.

Health centres and chemists

There are both Spanish national health system health centres (Centro de Salud) Saludrivate doctors and private health centres in Ibiza. The Centros de Salud accept the European Health Insurance Card (EHIC), so if you come from an EU country, you can be treated there for free. You need to present your card, so make sure to take it with you. If you go to a private doctor or health centre, you have to pay for the bill yourself, which you can reclaim if you have private health insurance. To make sure that you are reimbursed the whole amount and to cover against additional risks, such as transport back to your home country in case of severe illness or death, we recommend that you take out full travel insurance. There is always a chemist (farmacia) open 24 hours and the duty roster is posted on the doors of all other chemists. You will find that the chemists are excellent at recommending the equivalent of the medicine you take at home and offer good general advice.

Passport and safety

Your accommodation will require your passport or identity card for a maximum of 24 hours for registration purposes. You should also keep a copy of your identification with you at all times and leave the original in a safe place. Ibiza is generally considered a safe place to visit, but petty crimes like pick-pocketing and bag snatching can occur, especially in crowded areas or at night. You should keep your valuables locked away or carry them close to your body. You should also avoid political demonstrations and crowds, as they can turn violent or be targeted by terrorists. When enjoying the island's nightlife, you should keep an eye on your drinks and never accept drinks from strangers or leave them unattended. You should also never drink and drive or get into a car with someone who has been drinking. You should always use licensed taxis or public transport.

Vaccines and medicines

You should check the vaccines and medicines list on the CDC website and visit your doctor at least a month before your trip to get vaccines or medicines you may need. Some of these vaccines include COVID-19, hepatitis A, hepatitis B, measles-mumps-rubella (MMR), rabies and tetanus-diphtheria-pertussis (Tdap). You should also bring any prescription medicines you take regularly, as well as over-the-counter medicines such as painkillers, antihistamines, anti-diarrhoea pills and insect repellent.

Other risks

There are some other health and safety risks that you should be aware of when visiting Ibiza. These include:

Leptospirosis: This is a bacterial infection that can be contracted by touching urine or other body fluids from an animal infected with leptospirosis; swimming or wading in urine-contaminated fresh water; or drinking water or eating food contaminated with animal urine. Symptoms include fever, headache, muscle pain, vomiting and jaundice. You should avoid contaminated water and soil and seek medical attention if you develop symptoms.

Leishmaniasis: This is a parasitic infection that can be transmitted by the bite of a sand fly. Symptoms include skin ulcers, fever, weight loss and enlarged spleen and liver. You should avoid bug bites by wearing long-sleeved clothing, using insect repellent and sleeping under a mosquito net. You should also seek medical attention if you develop symptoms.

Hantavirus: This is a viral infection that can be spread by breathing in air or accidentally eating food contaminated with the urine, droppings or saliva of infected rodents; or by the bite of an infected rodent. Symptoms include fever, headache, muscle pain, coughing and shortness of breath. You should avoid rodents and areas where they live and seek medical attention if you develop symptoms.

Forest fires: Ibiza is prone to forest fires in the summer months due to the dry and hot weather. You should be careful when using fire or cigarettes in wooded areas and follow the instructions of the local authorities in case of a fire. You should also avoid driving or hiking in areas affected by fire and stay away from smoke.

Emergency Contacts

Ibiza is a beautiful and fun destination, but sometimes things can go wrong and you may need to contact the emergency services or other helpful organisations. Below are some emergency contacts that you should save on your phone or write down before you travel to Ibiza.

Emergency services

In case of an emergency, such as a fire, a crime, an accident or a medical problem, you can dial 112 from any phone. This is the pan-European emergency number that connects you to the police, the fire brigade or the ambulance service. You can also dial 061 for medical emergencies or 062 for the Civil Guard (a national police force). The operators speak Spanish and English, and sometimes other languages. You should explain your situation clearly and calmly, and provide your name, location and phone number.

Hospitals and health centres

There are both public and private hospitals and health centres in Ibiza. If you have a European Health Insurance Card (EHIC), you can access the public health system for free or at a reduced cost. You should present your card at the health centre or hospital. If you have private health insurance, you can go to a private doctor or health centre, but you will have to pay for the bill yourself and then claim it back from your insurance company. To make sure that you are fully covered and to avoid additional costs, we recommend that you take out full travel insurance before you travel to Ibiza. Below are some of the main hospitals and health centres in Ibiza:

Can Misses Hospital: This is the main public hospital in Ibiza. It is located in Ibiza Town and has an emergency department, an intensive care unit, a maternity ward, a paediatric ward and various specialities. The phone number is +34 971 397 000.

Policlinica del Rosario: This is a private hospital in Ibiza Town that offers various medical services, such as surgery, cardiology, dermatology, gynaecology, ophthalmology and more. The phone number is +34 971 301 916.

Cas Serrer: This is a public health centre in San Antonio that provides primary care, emergency care, paediatrics, dentistry and more. The phone number is +34 971 392 960.

Formentera Health Centre: This is the main public health centre in Formentera. It provides primary care, emergency care, radiology, laboratory and more. The phone number is +34 971 322 369.

Chemists

There are many chemists (farmacias) in Ibiza where you can buy medicines, toiletries and other products. Some of them are open 24 hours a day and have a green cross sign outside. The duty roster of the chemists is posted on the doors of all other chemists. You will find that the chemists are very helpful and can advise you on the best medicine for your condition or the equivalent of the medicine you take at home.

Consulates

If you need consular assistance during your stay in Ibiza, such as renewing your passport, reporting a lost or stolen document, getting legal advice or contacting your relatives in case of an emergency, you can contact your embassy or consulate in Ibiza or Madrid. Below are some of the consulates in Ibiza:

British Consulate: This is located in Ibiza Town and provides consular services to British nationals in Ibiza and Formentera. The phone number is +34 933 666 200 and the email address is spain.consulate@fco.gov.uk.

German Consulate: This is located in Ibiza Town and provides consular services to German nationals in Ibiza and Formentera. The phone number is +34 971 315 763 and the email address is ibiza@hk-diplo.de.

French Consulate: This is located in Ibiza Town and provides consular services to French nationals in Ibiza and Formentera. The phone number is +34 971 312 031.

Italian Consulate: This is located in Ibiza Town and provides consular services to Italian nationals in Ibiza and Formentera. The phone number is +34 971 199 915 and the email address is ibiza.onorario@esteri.it.

Other useful contacts

Below are some other useful contacts that you may need during your trip to Ibiza:

Tourist information: You can find tourist information offices in various locations in Ibiza where you can get maps, brochures, advice and recommendations on what to see and do on the island. The main tourist information office is located in Ibiza Town and the phone number is +34 971 302 490.

Taxi: You can find taxi ranks in various locations in Ibiza or you can call a taxi by phone. The main taxi company in Ibiza is Radio Taxi and the phone number is +34 971 398 483.

Bus: You can travel around Ibiza by bus using the public transport network. Various bus companies operate different routes and timetables. You can find more information on the websites of the bus companies.

Ferry: You can travel to and from Ibiza by ferry using various ferry companies that operate regular services to other Balearic islands, mainland Spain and other destinations. You can find more information on the websites of the ferry companies.

Communication and Internet Access

Ibiza is a well-connected island that offers various options for communication and internet access. Below are some tips to help you get connected to Ibiza.

Mobile phone

If you have a mobile phone from another EU country, you can use it in Ibiza without paying any roaming charges, thanks to the EU roaming regulation. However, if you have a mobile phone from a non-EU country, you may face high roaming fees or poor coverage. In that case, you may want to buy a local SIM card or a prepaid phone in Ibiza. You can find various mobile phone operators in Ibiza that offer different plans and rates, such as:

Simyo: This is an online-only operator that offers cheap and flexible plans for calls, texts and data. You can design your plan or choose from their pre-made options. You can order a SIM card online or buy one from their partner stores in Ibiza.

Suop: This is a user-owned operator that offers low-cost plans for calls, texts and data. You can choose from their monthly plans or pay-as-you-go options. You can order a SIM card online or buy one from their partner stores in Ibiza.

Yoigo: This is one of the main operators in Spain that offers competitive plans for calls, texts and data. You can choose from their contract plans or prepaid options. You can order a SIM card online or buy one from their stores in Ibiza.

You can also find other operators on Ibiza, such as MásMóvil, Movistar, Orange and Vodafone. You can compare their plans and rates online or visit their stores in Ibiza.

Landline phone

If you want to have a landline phone in your home in Ibiza, you will need to have a phone line installed and choose a provider. The main provider of phone lines in

Spain is Movistar, which is part of the Telefónica group. You can request a phone line installation online or by phone. The installation fee is around €100 and the monthly fee is around €15. You can also choose other providers that use Movistar's network, such as Orange or Vodafone. They may offer cheaper rates or bundle deals with internet and TV services.

To make local calls in Ibiza, you just need to dial the seven-digit number. To make national calls to other parts of Spain, you need to dial 9 followed by the nine-digit number. To make international calls, you need to dial 00 followed by the country code, area code and number.

Internet access

If you want to have internet access in your home in Ibiza, you will need to have a broadband connection installed and choose a provider. The main types of broadband connections available in Ibiza are:

Fibre optic: This is the fastest and most reliable type of broadband connection, but it is not available everywhere in Ibiza. You can check the coverage online or by phone with the providers that offer fibre optic services, such as Movistar, Orange or Vodafone.

ADSL: This is the most common type of broadband connection, but it is slower and less stable than fibre optic. It uses the existing phone line to deliver internet access. You can check the availability online or by phone with the providers that offer ADSL services, such as Movistar, Orange or Vodafone.

WiMAX: This is a wireless type of broadband connection that uses radio waves to deliver internet access. It does not require a phone line or cable installation, but it depends on the signal strength and weather conditions. You can check the coverage online or by phone with the providers that offer WiMAX services, such as ConectaBalear.

You can compare the plans and rates of different providers online or visit their stores in Ibiza. You can also find bundle deals that include internet, TV and landline phone services.

Wi-Fi access

If you don't want to have a fixed internet connection in your home in Ibiza, or if you just need occasional Wi-Fi access when you are out and about, you can find various options for Wi-Fi access in Ibiza:

Public Wi-Fi: You can find free public Wi-Fi hotspots

in various locations in Ibiza, such as airports, bus stations, tourist offices, libraries, parks and beaches. You may need to register with your email address or phone number to access them.

Cafés and restaurants: You can also find free Wi-Fi hotspots in many cafés and restaurants in Ibiza. You may need to ask for a password or buy something to access them.

Wi-Fi rental: You can rent a portable Wi-Fi device that provides unlimited internet access wherever you go in Ibiza. You can order it online or by phone and have it delivered to your accommodation or pick it up from a partner store in Ibiza. You can choose from different providers that offer Wi-Fi rental services, such as AlldayInternetSpain, My Webspot or Wifivox.

VPN access

If you want to access websites or content that are blocked or restricted in Spain, such as Netflix, Hulu or BBC iPlayer, you may need to use a VPN (Virtual Private Network) service. A VPN service allows you to connect to the internet through a secure and encrypted server in another country, thus bypassing the geo-restrictions and censorship. You can choose from different providers that offer VPN services, such as ExpressVPN, NordVPN or

Surfshark. You can download their apps on your devices and sign up for a subscription plan online.

Chapter 9 • Recommended Itineraries

3 Days in Ibiza for Party Lovers

Ibiza is the ultimate destination for party lovers who want to experience the best of the island's nightlife, music and culture. From world-famous clubs to beach bars, from boat parties to festivals, Ibiza has something for everyone who loves to dance, drink and have fun. Below is a suggested itinerary for 3 days in Ibiza for party lovers, covering some of the highlights of the island's party scene.

Day 1: Explore Ibiza Town and party at Pacha

On your first day, you can explore the capital of Ibiza, Ibiza Town, which is full of history, charm and character. You can wander around the old town, Dalt Vila, which is a UNESCO World Heritage Site. You can admire the views from the castle, visit the cathedral and the museums, and shop at the boutiques and markets. You can also enjoy the lively atmosphere of the port, where you can find many bars, restaurants and street performers.

In the evening, you can head to Pacha, one of the most iconic clubs in Ibiza. Pacha is open all year round and hosts some of the biggest names in electronic music, such as David Guetta, Calvin Harris, Solomun and more. You can dance the night away in one of the five rooms, each with a different music style and vibe. You can also chill out on the terrace or in the VIP area.

Day 2: Relax at a beach club and party at Ushuaïa

On your second day, you can relax and recover from the night before at one of the many beach clubs in Ibiza. You can choose from different options depending on your mood and budget, such as:

Blue Marlin: This is one of the most glamorous and exclusive beach clubs in Ibiza. It is located in Cala Jondal and attracts celebrities and jet-setters. You can enjoy the sun loungers, cabanas, pool, restaurant and bar. You can also listen to live DJs and bands that play from afternoon till night.

Nassau Beach Club: This is a chic and elegant beach club located in Playa den Bossa. It offers a relaxing and sophisticated atmosphere with comfortable sun beds, parasols, massage service, a restaurant and a bar. You can also enjoy live music and entertainment that varies from chill-out to house.

Bora Bora: This is one of the most famous and popular beach clubs in Ibiza. It is located in Playa d'en Bossa and attracts a young and fun crowd. You can party from day to night with loud music, dancing, drinks and shows. You can also access the beach and swim in the sea.

In the evening, you can continue the party at Ushuaïa, one of the most spectacular open-air clubs in Ibiza. Ushuaïa is located in Playa d'en Bossa and hosts some of the best pool parties on the island. You can enjoy amazing shows with dancers, performers, fireworks and lasers. You can also see some of the top DJs in the world, such as Martin Garrix, Armin van Buuren, Kygo and more.

Day 3: Join a boat party and party at Amnesia

On your third day, you can join a boat party and experience Ibiza from a different perspective. You can choose from different boat parties that offer different music styles, durations and routes. Some of the best boat parties in Ibiza are:

Cirque de la Nuit: This is one of the longest-running and most popular boat parties in Ibiza. It offers a 4-hour cruise with unlimited drinks, snacks, water sports and live DJs. It also includes entry to some of the best clubs in Ibiza.

Float Your Boat: This is another great option for boat parties in Ibiza. It offers a 3-hour cruise with free drinks, sunset views, swimming stops and live DJs. It also includes entry to some of the best clubs in Ibiza.

Pukka Up: This is one of the most glamorous and stylish boat parties in Ibiza. It offers a 3-hour cruise with free drinks, stunning views, swimming stops and live DJs. It also includes entry to some of the best clubs in Ibiza.

In the evening, you can end your trip with a bang at Amnesia, one of the most legendary clubs in Ibiza. Amnesia is located in San Rafael and has two massive rooms with state-of-the-art sound systems and lighting effects. You can dance till dawn with some of the best parties in Ibiza, such as Elrow, Cocoon, Together and more.

Tips for partying in Ibiza

Below are some tips to help you make the most of your party experience in Ibiza:

Plan: Ibiza is a very popular destination, especially in the summer months, so it is advisable to book your flights, accommodation, tickets and reservations in advance. You can also check the party calendar online to see what's on and who's playing.

Stay safe: Ibiza is generally a safe place, but you should still be careful and responsible when partying. You should drink plenty of water, avoid drugs and excessive alcohol, keep an eye on your belongings and never accept drinks from strangers or leave them unattended. You should also avoid driving or getting into a car with someone who has been drinking. You should always use licensed taxis or public transport.

Have fun: Ibiza is a place where you can have the time of your life, so don't be afraid to let loose and enjoy yourself. You can meet new people, make new friends, discover new music and create unforgettable memories. Ibiza is a place where anything can happen, so be open-minded and ready for surprises.

3 Days in Ibiza for Nature Lovers

Ibiza is not only a destination for party lovers, but also for nature lovers who want to explore the island's natural beauty, diversity and tranquillity. From stunning beaches and coves to lush forests and mountains, from salt flats and wetlands to caves and islands, Ibiza has something for everyone who loves to be in touch with nature. Below is a suggested itinerary for 3 days in Ibiza for nature lovers, covering some of the highlights of the island's natural wonders.

Day 1: Visit Ses Salines Natural Park and Es Vedrà

On your first day, you can visit Ses Salines Natural Park, a protected area that stretches from the south of Ibiza to the north of Formentera. This park is home to a variety of landscapes and ecosystems, such as dunes, pine forests, salt flats, lagoons and beaches. You can also find a rich biodiversity of flora and fauna, including endemic plants, migratory birds, reptiles and fish. You can explore the park by foot, bike or car, and enjoy the views, the scents and the sounds of nature.

In the afternoon, you can head to Cala d'Hort, a beautiful beach on the west coast of Ibiza that offers stunning views of Es Vedrà, a mysterious rocky island that rises from the sea. Es Vedrà is said to have mystical powers and legends, such as being the home of sirens, nymphs and giants. You can admire the island from the beach or a viewpoint from the cliffs. You can also take a boat trip to get closer to the island and see its impressive cliffs and caves.

Day 2: Explore Dalt Vila and Can Marçà Caves

On your second day, you can explore Dalt Vila, the old town of Ibiza that is a UNESCO World Heritage Site. Dalt Vila is surrounded by ancient walls and has a rich history and culture that dates back to Phoenician, Roman, Arab and Catalan times. You can wander around the narrow streets and alleys, visit the cathedral and the museums, shop at the markets and boutiques, and enjoy the views from the castle. You can also appreciate the architecture and the art that reflect the island's heritage.

In the evening, you can head to Port de Sant Miquel, a small bay on the north coast of Ibiza that hosts one of the island's natural treasures: Can Marçà Caves. These caves are an ancient smugglers' hideout that has been transformed into a spectacular attraction. You can take a guided tour through the caves and see the stalactites, stalagmites, waterfalls and lakes that create a magical atmosphere. You can also enjoy a light show that enhances the beauty of the caves.

Day 3: Hike to Sa Talaiassa mountain and relax at Cala Comte beach

On your third day, you can hike to Sa Talaiassa mountain, the highest point on Ibiza at 475 meters above sea level. This mountain is located in the southwest of Ibiza and offers panoramic views of the island and the sea. You can start your hike from Sant Josep de sa Talaia or Es Cubells, two charming villages that have churches, restaurants and shops. The hike is moderate and takes about 2 hours each way. You can enjoy the scenery along the way, such as pine forests, olive groves and almond trees.

In the afternoon, you can relax at Cala Comte Beach, one of the most beautiful beaches in Ibiza. This beach is located on the west coast of Ibiza and has crystal-clear water, golden sand and rocky islets. You can swim, snorkel or sunbathe on this beach or one of its smaller coves. You can also enjoy a drink or a meal at one of its beach bars or restaurants. You can also watch one of the most spectacular sunsets in Ibiza from this beach or a nearby viewpoint.

Tips for enjoying nature in Ibiza

Below are some tips to help you make the most of your nature experience in Ibiza:

Plan: Ibiza is a popular destination, especially in the summer months (June-September), so it is advisable to book your flights, accommodation, tickets and reservations in advance. You can also check online or ask locals for information about weather conditions (the average temperature in summer is 26°C), opening hours (some attractions may close in winter) and accessibility (some places may require a car or a boat).

Stay safe: Ibiza is generally a safe place but you should still be careful when enjoying nature. You should wear appropriate clothing (hat, sunglasses sunscreen), shoes (hiking boots or sandals) and equipment (water bottle, backpack, map) for your activities. You should also avoid going alone, respect the environment (don't litter, don't feed animals, don't pick plants) and follow the rules and signs of the places you visit.

Have fun: Ibiza is a place where you can have a wonderful time, so don't be afraid to try new things, meet new people and discover new places. You can find many opportunities to enjoy nature in Ibiza, such as kayaking, cycling, horse riding, diving and more. You can also join tours or groups that share your interests and passions. Ibiza is a place where you can connect with nature and yourself.

3 Days in Ibiza for Food Lovers

Ibiza is also for food lovers who want to taste the island's gastronomy, which reflects its history and diversity. From fresh seafood and local meats to pastries and cheeses, from traditional dishes and tapas to fusion cuisine and fine dining, Ibiza has something for everyone who loves to eat well. Below is a suggested itinerary for 3 days in Ibiza for food lovers, covering some of the highlights of the island's culinary scene.

Day 1: Try paella and hierbas ibicencas

On your first day, you can try one of the most emblematic dishes of Ibiza and the Balearic Islands: paella. This saffron-scented rice dish is usually cooked with local seafood, such as prawns, mussels, clams and squid, but you can also find other versions with meat or vegetables. You can enjoy paella at one of the many beach restaurants in Ibiza, such as:

Es Boldadó: This is a rustic and charming restaurant located in Cala d'Hort, with stunning views of Es Vedrà island. It offers a variety of paellas and other rice dishes, as well as grilled fish and salads.

Sa Nansa: This is a modern and elegant restaurant located in Ibiza Town, near the port. It offers a variety of paellas and other rice dishes, as well as seafood specialities, such as lobster stew or grilled octopus.

El Carmen: This is a cosy and friendly restaurant located in Cala d'Hort, with views of the beach and the sea. It offers a variety of paellas and other rice dishes, as well as tapas, salads and desserts.

After your paella feast, you can try one of the most typical drinks of Ibiza: hierbas ibicencas. This is a herbal liqueur made with aniseed and various plants that grow on the island, such as rosemary, thyme, fennel and mint. It has a sweet and aromatic taste and is usually served chilled or over ice as a digestive or a shot. You can find hierbas ibicencas at any bar or restaurant in Ibiza, or you can buy a bottle at one of the many shops that sell local products.

Day 2: Taste sofrit pagès and flaó

On your second day, you can taste one of the most traditional dishes of Ibiza: sofrit pagès. This is a hearty stew made with chicken, lamb, potatoes, garlic and various local sausages, such as sobrasada (a cured pork sausage seasoned with paprika) and butifarra (a fresh pork sausage seasoned with spices). It is cooked with olive oil, wine, saffron, cinnamon, cloves and parsley, creating a rich and fragrant sauce. You can find sofrit pagès at many restaurants in Ibiza that serve local cuisine, such as:

Es Rebost de Can Prats: This is a family-run restaurant located in Sant Antoni de Portmany, with a rustic and cosy atmosphere. It offers a variety of traditional dishes, such as sofrit pagès , bullit de peix (a fish stew with rice) and greixonera (a bread pudding with eggs, milk and cinnamon).

Ca n'Alfredo: This is one of the oldest restaurants in Ibiza, located in Ibiza Town near the port. It offers a variety of traditional dishes, such as sofrit pagès , arròs de matances (a rice dish with pork) and borrida de ratjada (a ray stew with almonds).

Es Ventall: This is a modern and stylish restaurant located in Sant Antoni de Portmany, with views of the bay. It offers a variety of traditional dishes with a creative twist, such as sofrit pagès , croquettes de bullit de peix (fish stew croquettes) and carpaccio de gamba roja (red shrimp carpaccio).

After your sofrit pagès , you can try one of the most typical desserts of Ibiza: flaó . This is a baked cheesecake made with fresh cheese (usually sheep's or goat's cheese), eggs, sugar, flour and mint leaves. It has a firm and crumbly texture and a refreshing and slightly tangy taste. You can find flaó at many bakeries, cafes and restaurants in Ibiza, or you can make it yourself with this recipe.

Day 3: Sample tapas and wine

On your third day, you can sample some of the best tapas and wine in Ibiza. Tapas are small dishes that are usually served as appetizers or snacks but can also make a full meal when ordered in larger quantities. You can find a variety of tapas in Ibiza, from traditional ones such as tortilla de patatas (potato omelette), croquetas (fried bechamel balls with ham, cheese or other fillings) and jamón ibérico (cured ham from black pigs), to more creative ones such as ensaladilla de pulpo (octopus salad), albóndigas de cordero (lamb meatballs) and patatas bravas con alioli (fried potatoes with spicy sauce and garlic mayonnaise). You can enjoy tapas at one of the many bars and restaurants in Ibiza that offer them, such as:

La Bodega: This is a lively and colourful tapas bar

located in Ibiza Town near the old town. It offers a variety of tapas and pinchos (small bites on bread), as well as salads, soups and desserts.

Can Terra: This is a cosy and friendly tapas bar located in Ibiza Town near the port. It offers a variety of tapas and pinchos, as well as cheese boards, charcuterie boards and desserts.

Tapas Restaurant & Lounge Bar: This is a chic and elegant tapas bar located in San Antonio de Portmany near the bay. It offers a variety of tapas and pinchos, as well as salads, burgers and desserts.

To accompany your tapas, you can try some of the best wines in Ibiza. Ibiza has a long tradition of wine-making that dates back to the Phoenician times. The island produces mainly white wines from local grape varieties such as malvasia, macabeo and moscatel, but also some red wines from varieties such as monastrell, tempranillo and syrah. You can find wine from Ibiza at any bar or restaurant on the island, or you can visit one of the many wineries that offer tours and tastings, such as:

Can Rich: This is an organic winery located in Sant Antoni de Portmany that produces wine, olive oil and hierbas ibicencas. It offers guided tours of the vineyards and the cellar, as well as tastings of its products.

Ibizkus: This is a modern winery located in Santa Eulària des Riu that produces wine from local and foreign grape varieties. It offers guided tours of the vineyards and the cellar, as well as tastings of its wines.

Sa Cova: This is a family-run winery located in Sant Mateu d'Albarca that produces wine from local grape varieties. It offers guided tours of the vineyards and the cellar, as well as tastings of its wines.

3 Days in Ibiza for Culture Lovers

Ibiza is also a destination for culture lovers who want to learn about the island's history and diversity. From ancient civilizations and medieval fortifications to hippie movements and artistic expressions, Ibiza has something for everyone who loves to discover new cultures. Below is a suggested itinerary for 3 days in Ibiza for culture lovers, covering some of the highlights of the island's cultural scene.

Day 1: Visit Dalt Vila and Necròpolis Puig des Molins

On your first day, you can visit Dalt Vila, the old town of

Ibiza that is a UNESCO World Heritage Site. Dalt Vila is surrounded by ancient walls and has a rich history and culture that dates back to Phoenician, Roman, Arab and Catalan times. You can wander around the narrow streets and alleys, visit the cathedral and the museums, shop at the markets and boutiques, and enjoy the views from the castle. You can also appreciate the architecture and the art that reflect the island's heritage.

In the afternoon, you can head to Necròpolis Puig des Molins, another UNESCO World Heritage Site that reveals Ibiza's Phoenician roots. This is an archaeological site that contains more than 3,000 tombs from the 7th century BC to the 2nd century AD. You can see the different types of burials, such as hypogea (underground chambers), sarcophagi (stone coffins) and urns (clay vessels). You can also visit the museum that displays some of the artefacts found in the necropolis, such as jewellery, pottery and figurines.

Day 2: Explore the hippie market and the contemporary art museum

On your second day, you can explore one of the most iconic aspects of Ibiza's culture: the hippie market. The hippie market is a colourful and lively place where you can find a variety of handmade goods, such as clothes, accessories, jewellery, art and crafts. You can also enjoy live music, street performers and food stalls. The hippie market is held every Wednesday in Es Canar and every Saturday in Sant Carles de Peralta.

In the evening, you can head to the Museu d'Art Contemporani d'Eivissa (MACE), the contemporary art museum of Ibiza2. This museum is set in a converted 18th-century building in Dalt Vila and hosts excellent temporary exhibitions of local and international artists. You can see works of different styles and mediums, such as painting, sculpture, photography and video. You can also admire the architecture and design of the museum itself, which combines old and new elements.

Day 3: Take a day trip to Formentera and enjoy a traditional dinner

On your third day, you can take a day trip to Formentera, the smallest and most peaceful of the Balearic Islands. You can take a ferry from Ibiza Town or Playa d'en Bossa and reach Formentera in about 30 minutes. You can explore this island by bike or scooter and discover its natural beauty, such as white sandy beaches, turquoise water, salt flats and lighthouses. You can also visit its charming villages, such as Sant Francesc Xavier, Sant Ferran de Ses Roques and El Pilar de la Mola.

In the evening, you can return to Ibiza and enjoy a traditional dinner at one of its restaurants that serve local cuisine. You can try dishes such as sofrit pagès (a stew of meat, potatoes and sausages), bullit de peix (a fish stew with rice), greixonera (a bread pudding with eggs, milk and cinnamon) and flaó (a baked cheesecake with cheese and mint). You can also drink wine from Ibiza or hierbas ibicencas (a herbal liqueur).

Tips for enjoying culture in Ibiza

Below are some tips to help you make the most of your cultural experience in Ibiza:

Plan: Ibiza is a popular destination, especially in the summer months (June-September), so it is advisable to book your flights, accommodation, tickets and reservations in advance. You can also check online or ask locals for information about opening hours (some attractions may close in winter), entrance fees (some attractions may charge admission) and events (some attractions may host special events).

Stay curious: Ibiza has a lot of culture to offer, so don't be afraid to explore new places, learn new things and meet new people. You can find many opportunities to enjoy culture in Ibiza, such as festivals, concerts, workshops and tours. You can also join groups or clubs that share your interests and passions.

Respect diversity: Ibiza is a place where you can find a variety of cultures, languages and lifestyles, so be respectful and tolerant of the differences and similarities. You can also appreciate the diversity and richness of Ibiza's culture, which is influenced by its history, geography and people.

3 Days in Ibiza for Couples

Ibiza is a perfect destination for couples who want to enjoy a romantic getaway with a mix of relaxation, adventure and fun. The island offers stunning beaches, charming villages, scenic views and a vibrant nightlife that can suit any mood and taste. Below is a suggested itinerary for 3 days in Ibiza for couples, covering some of the best activities and places to visit on the island.

Day 1: Relax at a beach club and watch the sunset

On your first day, you can relax and unwind at one of the

many beach clubs in Ibiza, where you can enjoy the sun, the sea and the music. You can choose from different options depending on your style and budget, such as:

Nikki Beach: This is one of the most glamorous and exclusive beach clubs in Ibiza. It is located in Santa Eulària des Riu and attracts celebrities and jet-setters. You can enjoy the sun loungers, cabanas, pool, restaurant and bar. You can also listen to live DJs and entertainment that vary from chill-out to house.

Cotton Beach Club: This is a chic and elegant beach club located in Cala Tarida. It offers a relaxing and sophisticated atmosphere with comfortable sun beds, parasols, massage service, a restaurant and a bar. You can also enjoy panoramic views of the sea and the sunset.

Benirrás Beach: This is one of the most famous and popular beaches in Ibiza. It is located in the north of the island and attracts a bohemian and hippie crowd. You can party from day to night with drums, dancing, drinks and shows. You can also access the beach and swim in the sea.

In the evening, you can head to one of the best spots to watch the sunset on Ibiza, which is one of the most romantic things to do on the island. You can choose from different locations depending on your preference, such as:

Cala Comte: This is one of the most beautiful beaches in Ibiza. It is located on the west coast of the island and has crystal-clear water, golden sand and rocky islets. You can swim, snorkel or sunbathe on this beach or one of its smaller coves. You can also enjoy a drink or a meal at one of its beach bars or restaurants.

San Antonio's Sunset Strip: This is one of the most iconic places to watch the sunset in Ibiza. It is located in San Antonio de Portmany and has a lively and festive atmosphere. You can find many bars, restaurants and street performers along this strip. You can also join the crowds that clap and cheer as the sun dips into the sea.

Es Vedrà: This is one of the most mysterious and mystical places in Ibiza. It is a rocky island that rises from the sea off the coast of Cala d'Hort. It is said to have magical powers and legends, such as being the home of sirens, nymphs and giants. You can admire the island from a viewpoint on the cliffs or from a boat trip.

Day 2: Explore Dalt Vila and enjoy a fine dining experience

On your second day, you can explore Dalt Vila, the old

town of Ibiza that is a UNESCO World Heritage Site. Dalt Vila is surrounded by ancient walls and has a rich history and culture that dates back to Phoenician, Roman, Arab and Catalan times. You can wander around the narrow streets and alleys, visit the cathedral and the museums, shop at the markets and boutiques, and enjoy the views from the castle. You can also appreciate the architecture and the art that reflect the island's heritage.

In the evening, you can treat yourself to a fine dining experience at one of Ibiza's top restaurants, where you can taste some of the best dishes and wines on the island. You can choose from different options depending on your palate and occasion, such as:

Sublimotion: This is one of the most innovative and expensive restaurants in the world. It is located in Playa d'en Bossa inside Hard Rock Hotel Ibiza. It offers a 20-course tasting menu that combines gastronomy, technology, art and entertainment. You can experience a multisensory journey that stimulates all your senses.

Heart Ibiza: This is one of the most creative and eclectic restaurants in Ibiza. It is located in Marina Botafoch near Ibiza Town. It is a collaboration between

Ferran Adrià (one of the world's best chefs) and Cirque du Soleil (one of the world's best entertainment companies). You can enjoy a fusion of food, music, art and performance.

La Gaia: This is one of the most elegant and refined restaurants in Ibiza. It is located in Ibiza Town inside Gran Hotel Ibiza. It offers a fusion of Mediterranean and Japanese cuisine, with dishes such as sushi, sashimi, ceviche and tiradito. You can also enjoy a selection of cocktails and wines.

Day 3: Take a day trip to Formentera and enjoy a traditional dinner

On your third day, you can take a day trip to Formentera, the smallest and most peaceful of the Balearic Islands. You can take a ferry from Ibiza Town or Playa d'en Bossa and reach Formentera in about 30 minutes. You can explore this island by bike or scooter and discover its natural beauty, such as white sandy beaches, turquoise water, salt flats and lighthouses. You can also visit its charming villages, such as Sant Francesc Xavier, Sant Ferran de Ses Roques and El Pilar de la Mola.

In the evening, you can return to Ibiza and enjoy a

traditional dinner at one of its restaurants that serve local cuisine. You can try dishes such as sofrit pagès (a stew of meat, potatoes and sausages), bullit de peix (a fish stew with rice), greixonera (a bread pudding with eggs, milk and cinnamon) and flaó (a baked cheesecake with cheese and mint). You can also drink wine from Ibiza or hierbas ibicencas (a herbal liqueur). You can find these dishes at many restaurants in Ibiza, such as:

Es Rebost de Can Prats: This is a family-run restaurant located in Sant Antoni de Portmany, with a rustic and cosy atmosphere. It offers a variety of traditional dishes, such as sofrit pagès , bullit de peix and greixonera.

Ca n'Alfredo: This is one of the oldest restaurants in Ibiza, located in Ibiza Town near the port. It offers a variety of traditional dishes, such as sofrit pagès , arròs de matances (a rice dish with pork) and borrida de ratjada (a ray stew with almonds).

Es Ventall: This is a modern and stylish restaurant located in Sant Antoni de Portmany, with views of the bay. It offers a variety of traditional dishes with a creative twist, such as sofrit pagès, croquettes de bullit de peix (fish stew croquettes) and carpaccio de gamba roja (red shrimp carpaccio).

Chapter 10 • Travelling with Children

Family-Friendly Attractions

Ibiza is a great destination for families who want to have fun and enjoy the island's natural and cultural attractions. There are many activities and places to visit that are suitable for children and adults of all ages. Below are some of the best family-friendly attractions in Ibiza:

Beaches

One of the main attractions of Ibiza is its beautiful beaches, where you can swim, sunbathe, play and relax. Many beaches in Ibiza are family-friendly, meaning that they have calm water, soft sand, lifeguards, facilities and services. Some of the best family-friendly beaches in Ibiza are:

Cala Llonga: This is a wide and shallow beach located in a sheltered bay on the east coast of Ibiza. It has clear water, fine sand and a playground. It also has many bars, restaurants and shops nearby.

Cala Tarida: This is a long and sandy beach located on

the west coast of Ibiza. It has turquoise water, rocky coves and a diving school. It also has many sunbeds, parasols and water sports available.

Portinatx: This is a small and picturesque beach located in the north of Ibiza. It has crystal water, white sand and a lighthouse. It also has many activities, such as kayaking, snorkelling and boat trips.

Boat trips

Another way to enjoy Ibiza's coastline is by taking a boat trip that allows you to see different places and islands from the sea. Many boat trips to Ibiza are family-friendly, meaning that they have comfortable and safe boats, friendly and professional staff, and entertainment and snacks on board. Some of the best family-friendly boat trips in Ibiza are:

Baleària: This is a ferry company that offers regular services to Formentera, the smallest and most peaceful of the Balearic Islands. You can take a ferry from Ibiza Town or Playa d'en Bossa and reach Formentera in about 30 minutes. You can explore this island by bike or scooter and discover its natural beauty.

Capitan Nemo: This is a boat company that offers various excursions to different locations in Ibiza, such as Aquarium + Cala Salada or Es Vedra. You can take a boat from San Antonio and enjoy the views, the music and the commentary. You can also swim, snorkel or visit the aquarium.

Santa Eulalia Ferry: This is a boat company that offers a scenic cruise along the east coast of Ibiza. You can take a boat from Santa Eulalia or Es Canar and see different beaches, coves and cliffs. You can also stop at Cala Llonga or Cala Pada for swimming or sunbathing.

Museums

If you want to learn more about Ibiza's history, culture and art, you can visit some of its family-friendly museums, meaning they have interesting exhibits, interactive displays and educational activities. Some of the best family-friendly museums in Ibiza are:

Museu d'Etnografia d'Eivissa: This is an ethnographic museum that showcases the traditional life and customs of Ibiza. It is located in an old farmhouse in Santa Eulalia and has various rooms with objects, tools and costumes. It also has a garden with plants and animals.

Museu Puget: This is an art museum that displays the works of two local painters: Narcís Puget Viñas and **Narcís Puget Riquer.** It is located in a historic building in Dalt Vila and has various rooms with paintings, drawings and sculptures. It also has a terrace with views.

Museu de la Mar: This is a maritime museum that tells the story of Ibiza's relationship with the sea. It is located in an old defence tower in Sant Antoni de Portmany and has various rooms with models, maps and photos. It also has a lookout point with views.

Child-Friendly Accommodation

Ibiza is an island with a variety of accommodation options that are child-friendly, meaning that they have facilities, services and activities that cater to the needs and preferences of the little ones. Below are some of the best child-friendly accommodations in Ibiza:

Hotels

If you prefer to stay in a hotel that provides all the amenities and comforts you need, you can choose from many hotels in Ibiza that are child-friendly, such as:

Hotel Vibra Vila: This is a central and modern hotel located in Ibiza Town, near Figueretas Beach. It has a rooftop pool and terrace with stunning sea views, as well as a TV lounge with a pool table. The rooms are spacious and air-conditioned, with satellite TV, a mini fridge and a private bathroom. The hotel also serves a buffet breakfast and has free WiFi. The hotel is close to many shops, bars and restaurants, as well as the port and the old town.

Hotel Ibiza Playa: This is a beachfront and elegant hotel located in Ibiza Town, near Playa d'en Bossa. It has a swimming pool with a children's section, as well as a restaurant and a bar. The rooms are bright and comfortable, with satellite TV, safe and private bathrooms. Some also have a private balcony with views of the sea and the island of Formentera. The hotel also offers free WiFi and bike rental. The hotel is close to many attractions, such as Space Nightclub, Bora Bora Beach Club and Ushuaïa.

TUI Blue Aura: This is an all-inclusive and spectacular hotel located in Port Des Torrent, near San Antonio Bay. It has an indoor swimming pool, splash park, baby pool and shaded children's pool, as well as free access to the waterpark next door. It also has a soft play area, playground, Baby Lounge and BabyClub. The rooms are stylish and spacious, with air-conditioning, satellite TV, a mini fridge and a private bathroom. Some also have a balcony or terrace with views of the pool or the sea. The hotel also offers free WiFi and entertainment.

Apartments

If you prefer to stay in an apartment that gives you more space and flexibility, you can choose from many apartments in Ibiza that are child-friendly, such as:

Balansat Resort: This is a resort that offers apartments located in Puerto De San Miguel, near the beach. It has a kid's splash park with little waterslides, sprinklers and fountains, as well as a swimming pool with a children's section. It also has a playground and an entertainment programme. The apartments are modern and practical, with air-conditioning, satellite TV, a kitchenette and a private bathroom. Some also have a balcony or terrace with views of the sea or the garden. The resort also has two restaurants with stunning sea views.

Casa Luis Apartments: This is a family-run complex that offers apartments located in Santa Eulalia, near the beach and the resort centre. It has two swimming pools with kids' sections, as well as a cute little splash park for water babies. It also has a playground and a great entertainment programme. The apartments are cosy and friendly, with air-conditioning, satellite TV, a kitchenette and a private bathroom. Some also have a balcony or terrace with views of the pool or the garden. The complex also has a bar with an outdoor terrace.

Playa Bella Apartments: This is an award-winning complex that offers apartments located in San Antonio Bay, on the beachfront. It has a children's swimming pool with a shipwreck and waterslides, as well as sunbeds, parasols and water sports available. It also has two restaurants with sea views and children's menus. The apartments are bright and spacious, with air-conditioning, satellite TV a, kitchenette and a private bathroom. Some also have a balcony or terrace with views of the sea or the garden.

Villas

If you prefer to stay in a villa that gives you more privacy and luxury, you can choose from many villas in Ibiza that are child-friendly, such as:

Villa Can Toni: This is a beautiful villa located in Sant Josep de sa Talaia, near Cala Tarida beach. It has a private swimming pool with sunbeds and parasols, as well as a barbecue area and a garden. It also has toys, books and games for children. The villa is spacious and stylish, with air-conditioning, satellite TV, a DVD player, a fully equipped kitchen and a private bathroom. It also has a terrace with views of the countryside and the sea.

The villa can accommodate up to 10 people in 5 bedrooms.

Villa Cana Maria: This is a charming villa located in Santa Eulalia, near Es Canar Beach. It has a private swimming pool with sunbeds and parasols, as well as a barbecue area and a garden. It also has a playground and a trampoline for children. The villa is cosy and rustic, with air-conditioning, satellite TV, a CD player, a fully equipped kitchen and a private bathroom. It also has a porch with views of the countryside. The villa can accommodate up to 8 people in 4 bedrooms.

Villa Cana Pepa: This is a stunning villa located in Sant Antoni de Portmany, near Cala Salada beach. It has a private swimming pool with sunbeds and parasols, as well as a barbecue area and a garden. It also has toys, books and games for children. The villa is modern and elegant, with air-conditioning, satellite TV, a DVD player, a fully equipped kitchen and a private bathroom. It also has a balcony with views of the sea. The villa can accommodate up to 10 people in 5 bedrooms.

Agritourism

If you prefer to stay in an agritourism that gives you more contact with nature and local culture, you can choose from many agritourism on Ibiza that are child-friendly, such as:

Agroturismo Can Guillem: This is an organic agritourism that offers rooms located in Ibiza Town, near the airport. It has a swimming pool with sunbeds and parasols, as well as a barbecue area and a garden. It also has animals, such as horses, donkeys and chickens. The rooms are spacious and comfortable, with air-conditioning, satellite TV, a mini fridge and a private bathroom. Some also have a balcony or terrace with views of the countryside. The agritourism also serves breakfast and dinner with local products.

Agroturismo Ca n'Escandell: This is a family-run agritourism that offers rooms located in Sant Joan de Labritja, near Portinatx Beach. It has a swimming pool with sunbeds and parasols, as well as a barbecue area and a garden. It also has animals, such as dogs, cats and sheep. The rooms are cosy and traditional, with air-conditioning, satellite TV, a mini fridge and a private bathroom. Some also have a fireplace or a terrace with views of the countryside. The agritourism also serves breakfast and dinner with local products.

Agroturismo Atzaró: This is a luxury agritourism that offers rooms located in Santa Eulalia, near Cala Nova beach. It has a swimming pool with sunbeds and parasols, as well as a spa area and a garden. It also has activities, such as yoga, meditation and cooking classes. The rooms are stylish and spacious, with air-conditioning, satellite TV, a minibar and a private bathroom. Some also have a jacuzzi or a terrace with views of the countryside. The agritourism also serves breakfast and dinner with local products.

Chapter 11 • Travelling on a Budget

Budget-Friendly Accommodation

Ibiza is a wonderful destination for travellers who want to enjoy the island's beauty, culture and nightlife without spending a fortune. The island offers a variety of accommodation options that are budget-friendly, meaning that they have low prices, good locations and decent facilities. Below are some of the best budget-friendly accommodations in Ibiza:

Hostels

If you prefer to stay in a hostel that provides a social and fun atmosphere, you can choose from many hostels in Ibiza that are budget-friendly, such as:

Amistat Island Hostel Ibiza: This is a new and modern hostel located in Sant Antoni de Portmany, near the beach and the bus station. It has dorms and private rooms with air-conditioning, lockers and a private bathroom. It also has a swimming pool, a terrace, a kitchen, a bar and a lounge. It offers free WiFi, breakfast and activities.

Hostal Florencio: This is a cosy and friendly hostel located in Sant Antoni de Portmany, near the port and the Sunset Strip. It has private rooms with air-conditioning, TV and a private bathroom. Some also have a balcony with views of the sea or the town. It also has a swimming pool, a restaurant, a bar and a bike rental service. It offers free WiFi and breakfast.

Hostal Residencia Rita: This is a family-run hostel located in Santa Eulalia del Rio, near the beach and the promenade. It has private rooms with air-conditioning, TV and a private bathroom. Some also have a balcony with views of the sea or the garden. It also has a terrace, a snack bar and a laundry service. It offers free WiFi.

Guesthouses

If you prefer to stay in a guesthouse that provides a more personal and intimate experience, you can choose from many guesthouses in Ibiza that are budget-friendly, such as:

Hostal La Torre: This is a charming and romantic guesthouse located in Sant Antoni de Portmany, on the cliffs overlooking the sea. It has private rooms with air-conditioning, TV and a private bathroom. Some also have a terrace with views of the sea and the sunset. It also has a restaurant, a bar and a garden. It offers free WiFi.

Casa Luisa: This is a lovely and rustic guesthouse located in Sant Joan de Labritja, in the countryside surrounded by nature. It has private rooms with air-conditioning, TV and a private bathroom. Some also have a fireplace or a terrace with views of the mountains or the fields. It also has an outdoor pool, a barbecue area and a garden. It offers free WiFi and breakfast.

Casa Naya: This is a beautiful and peaceful guesthouse located in Sant Llorenç de Balàfia, in the heart of Ibiza. It has private rooms with air-conditioning, TV and a private bathroom. Some also have a jacuzzi or a terrace with views of the pool or the countryside. It also has an indoor pool, an outdoor pool, a spa area and a garden. It offers free WiFi and breakfast.

Hotels

If you prefer to stay in a hotel that provides more comfort and convenience, you can choose from many hotels in Ibiza that are budget-friendly, such as:

Hotel Vibra Vila: This is one of our predefined tools' results for budget-friendly hotels in Ibiza.

Hotel Ibiza Playa: This is another one of our predefined tools' results for budget-friendly hotels in

Ibiza.

TUI Blue Aura: This is another one of our predefined tools' results for budget-friendly hotels in Ibiza.

Apartments

If you prefer to stay in an apartment that gives you more space and flexibility, you can choose from many apartments in Ibiza that are budget-friendly, such as:

Balansat Resort: This is one of our predefined tools' results for budget-friendly apartments in Ibiza.

Casa Luis Apartments: This is another one of our predefined tools' results for budget-friendly apartments in Ibiza.

Playa Bella Apartments: This is another one of our predefined tools' results for budget-friendly apartments in Ibiza.

Cheap Eats and Local Food

From fresh seafood and local meats to pastries and cheeses, from traditional dishes and tapas to fusion cuisine and fine dining, Ibiza has something for everyone who loves to eat well. And the best part is that you don't have to break the bank to enjoy it. There are many places in Ibiza where you can find cheap eats and local food that are delicious, authentic and satisfying. Below are some of the best cheap eats and local food in Ibiza:

Tapas

Tapas are small dishes that are usually served as appetizers or snacks but can also make a full meal when ordered in larger quantities. You can find a variety of tapas in Ibiza, from traditional ones such as tortilla de patatas (potato omelette), croquetas (fried bechamel balls with ham, cheese or other fillings) and jamón ibérico (cured ham from black pigs), to more creative ones such as ensaladilla de pulpo (octopus salad), albóndigas de cordero (lamb meatballs) and patatas bravas con alioli (fried potatoes with spicy sauce and garlic mayonnaise). You can enjoy tapas at one of the many bars and restaurants in Ibiza that offer them, such as:

La Bodega: This is a lively and colourful tapas bar located in Ibiza Town near the old town. It offers a variety of tapas and pinchos (small bites on bread), as well as salads, soups and desserts.

Can Terra: This is a cosy and friendly tapas bar located in Ibiza Town near the port. It offers a variety of tapas and pinchos, as well as cheese boards, charcuterie boards and desserts.

Tapas Restaurant & Lounge Bar: This is a chic and elegant tapas bar located in San Antonio de Portmany near the bay. It offers a variety of tapas and pinchos, as well as salads, burgers and desserts.

Pizza

Pizza is one of the most popular and affordable foods in Ibiza, where you can find many places that serve it with different toppings, sizes and styles. You can choose from classic Italian pizza with thin crust and tomato sauce, or more exotic pizza with thick crust and cheese sauce. You can also customize your pizza with your favourite ingredients, such as ham, cheese, mushrooms, peppers, olives, pineapple, chicken, tuna, etc. You can enjoy pizza at one of the many pizzerias in Ibiza that offer it, such as:

Pizzaman: This is one of the best pizzerias in Ibiza that offers authentic Italian pizza with fresh ingredients and homemade dough. It is located in Sant Antoni de Portmany near the beach. It offers a variety of pizzas with different sizes and toppings, as well as salads, pasta and desserts. It also has gluten-free options.

La Fraschetta Romana: This is another great pizzeria in Ibiza that offers tasty Italian pizza with quality ingredients and a crispy crust. It is located in Ibiza Town near the port. It offers a variety of pizzas with different sizes and toppings, as well as salads, pasta and desserts. It also has vegan options.

La Vela Pizzeria Ristorante Italiano: This is another excellent pizzeria in Ibiza that offers delicious Italian pizza with fresh ingredients and a soft crust. It is located in Santa Eulalia del Rio near the beach. It offers a variety of pizzas with different sizes and toppings, as well as salads, pasta and desserts. It also has vegetarian options.

Local cuisine

If you want to try some of the local cuisine of Ibiza, which is influenced by its Mediterranean climate, its agricultural products and its cultural heritage, you can find many places that serve it with reasonable prices and generous portions. You can try dishes such as sofrit pagès (a stew of meat, potatoes and sausages), bullit de peix (a fish stew with rice), greixonera (a bread pudding with eggs, milk and cinnamon) and flaó (a baked cheesecake with cheese and mint). You can enjoy local cuisine at one of the many restaurants in Ibiza that serve it, such as:

Es Rebost de Can Prats: This is a family-run

restaurant located in Sant Antoni de Portmany, with a rustic and cosy atmosphere. It offers a variety of traditional dishes, such as sofrit pagès , bullit de peix and greixonera.

Ca n'Alfredo: This is one of the oldest restaurants in Ibiza, located in Ibiza Town near the port. It offers a variety of traditional dishes, such as sofrit pagès , arròs de matances (a rice dish with pork) and borrida de ratjada (a ray stew with almonds).

Es Ventall: This is a modern and stylish restaurant located in Sant Antoni de Portmany, with views of the bay. It offers a variety of traditional dishes with a creative twist, such as sofrit pagès , croquettes de bullit de peix (fish stew croquettes) and carpaccio de gamba roja (red shrimp carpaccio).

Free and Affordable Attractions

The island offers many attractions that are free or affordable, meaning that they have no or low entrance fees, transportation costs or other expenses. Below are some of the best free and affordable attractions in Ibiza:

Nature

One of the main attractions of Ibiza is its natural

scenery, where you can admire the stunning beaches, cliffs, islands and countryside. There are many places in Ibiza where you can enjoy nature for free or for a small fee, such as:

Es Vedrà: This is one of the most mysterious and mystical places in Ibiza. It is a rocky island that rises from the sea off the coast of Cala d'Hort. It is said to have magical powers and legends, such as being the home of sirens, nymphs and giants. You can admire the island from a viewpoint on the cliffs or from a boat trip.

Cala Comte: This is one of the most beautiful beaches in Ibiza. It is located on the west coast of the island and has crystal-clear water, golden sand and rocky islets. You can swim, snorkel or sunbathe on this beach or one of its smaller coves. You can also enjoy a drink or a meal at one of its beach bars or restaurants.

Santa Gertrudis: This is one of the most charming villages in Ibiza. It is located in the centre of the island and has a rural and bohemian atmosphere. You can stroll around its square and streets, visit its church and shops, and taste its local products, such as cheese, honey and wine.

History

If you want to learn more about Ibiza's history, which

dates back to ancient civilizations and medieval times, you can visit some of its historical sites that are free or affordable, such as:

Dalt Vila: This is the old town of Ibiza that is a UNESCO World Heritage Site. Dalt Vila is surrounded by ancient walls and has a rich history and culture that dates back to Phoenician, Roman, Arab and Catalan times. You can wander around the narrow streets and alleys, visit the cathedral and the museums, shop at the markets and boutiques, and enjoy the views from the castle.

Necròpolis Puig des Molins: This is another UNESCO World Heritage Site that reveals Ibiza's Phoenician roots. This is an archaeological site that contains more than 3,000 tombs from the 7th century BC to the 2nd century AD. You can see the different types of burials, such as hypogea (underground chambers), sarcophagi (stone coffins) and urns (clay vessels). You can also visit the museum that displays some of the artefacts found in the necropolis.

Torre de ses Portes: This is one of the many defence towers that were built in Tipsbiza in the 16th century to protect the island from pirate attacks. It is located on the south coast of Ibiza near Ses Salines beach. It offers panoramic views of the sea and the island of Formentera.

Art

If you want to appreciate some of Ibiza's art, inich reflects its creativity and diversity, you can visit some of its art venues that are free or affordable, such as:

Museu d'Art Contemporani d'Eivissa (MACE): This is the contemporary art museum of Ibiza. It is set in a converted 18th-century building in Dalt Vila and hosts excellent temporary exhibitions of local and international artists. You can see works of different styles and mediums, such as painting, sculpture, photography and video. You can also admire the architecture and design of the museum itself, which combines old and new elements.

Feria de Navidad de Ibiza: This is a Christmas fair that takes place every year in Ibiza Town from December to January. It offers a variety of handmade goods, such as clothes, accessories, jewellery, art and crafts. You can also enjoy live music, street performers and food stalls.

Cala Olivera: This is a hidden beach that has become an open-air gallery for street art. It is located on the east coast of Ibiza near the Roca Llisa golf course. It has graffiti murals that cover the walls of a travelling building that used to be a military bunker. You can also swim in the water or relax on the pebbly sand.

Entertainment

If you want to have some fun and enjoy Ibiza's nightlife, which is famous for its clubs, bars and parties, you can find some of its entertainment options that are free or affordable, such as:

San Antonio's Sunset Strip: This is one of the most itravellersces to watch the sunset in Ibiza. It is located in San Antonio de Portmany and has a lively and festive atmosphere. You can find many bars, restaurants and street performers along this strip. You can also join the crowds that clap and cheer as the sun dips into the sea.

Benirrás Beach: This is one of the most famous and popular beaches in Ibiza. It is located in the north of the island and attracts a bohemian and hippie crowd. You can party from day to night with drums, dancing, drinks and shows. You can also access the beach and swim in the sea.

Pizzaman: This is one of the best pizzerias in Ibiza that also offers live music and karaoke nights. It is located in Sant Antoni de Portmany near the beach. It offers a variety of pizzas with different sizes and toppings, as well as salads, pasta and desserts. It also has gluten-free options.

Transportation Tips for Saving Money

Ibiza is a relatively small island, but it has many different places to visit and explore. Therefore, transportation is an important factor to consider when planning your trip and budget. There are various modes of transportation in Ibiza, such as buses, taxis, ferries, bikes and cars. However, some of them can be quite expensive or inconvenient, especially during the peak season (June-September). Below are some tips to help you save money and time on transportation in Ibiza:

Use the bus

The bus is one of the cheapest and easiest ways to get around Ibiza. There are regular bus services that connect the main towns, resorts and beaches on the island. You can buy single tickets or multi-trip passes at the bus stations or on bkilometresprices vary depending on the distance and the season, but they are usually between 1.55€ and 4€ per trip. You can also use the Disco Bus, a special night servicosyhat runs from midnight to 6 am and connects the main clubs and nightlife areas in Ibiza.

The price is 4€ per trip. You can check the bus timetables and routes online or at the bus stations.

Share a taxi

A taxi is a convenient and fast way to get to your destination in Ibiza, especially if you are travelling in a group or at night. However, taxis can be quite expensive in Ibiza, especially during the peak season or from/to the airport. The minimum fare is 3.65€ and the price per kilometer is 1.09€ during the day and 1.33€ during the night. There are also exa memorable times in special services. Therefore, it is advisable to share a taxi with other travellers if possible or to use a taxi app such as TaxiIbiza or Ibiza Taxi that allows you to book and pay for your taxi online.

Take a ferry

A ferry is a cosy and scenic way to travel between Ibiza and Formentera, the smallest and most peaceful of the Balearic Islands. You can take a ferry from Ibiza Town or Playa d'en Bossa and reach Formentera in about 30 minutes. You can explore this island by bike or scooter and discover its natural beauty, such as white sandy beaches, turquoise water, salt flats and lighthouses. The price of a ferry ticket varies depending on the company and the season, but it is usually between 19€ and 25€ for a round trip. You can also take a ferry to other destinations in Ibiza, such as a memorable Vedrà.

Rent a bike

A bike is an eco-friendly and healthy way to explore Ibiza at your own pace. You can rent a bike from one of the many bike rental shops in Ibiza, such as Kandani, Velo Club Ibiza or Bike Ibiza. The price of renting a bike depends on the type of bike, the duration and the season, but it is usually between 10€ and 20€ per day. You can also join guided bike tours that take you to different places on Ibiza, such as Dalt Vila, Santa Eulalia or Benirrás.

Hire a car

A car is an option for those who want more freedom and flexibility to travel around Ibiza. However, hiring a car can be quite costly on Ibiza, especially during the peak season or for longer periods. The price of hiring a car depends on the type of car, the duration, the insurance and the season, but it is usually between 30€ and 60€ per day. You also have to pay for fuel, parking and tolls. Therefore, it is advisable to compare different car rental companies online or at the airport before booking your car. You can also look for deals or discounts that include free kilometres, insurance or extras.

Conclusion

Ibiza is a destination that has something for everyone, whether you are looking for relaxation, adventure, culture or fun. The island offers a variety of attractions and activities that can suit any mood and taste, from stunning beaches and scenic views to historical sites and art venues, from traditional dishes and local products to fusion cuisine and fine dining, from peaceful villages and nature trails to lively clubs and parties. You can also enjoy the island's diversity and richness, which is influenced by its history, geography and people.

Ibiza is also a destination that can fit any budget, whether you are looking for luxury or affordability. The island offers a variety of accommodation options that can cater to your needs and preferences, from hotels and apartments to villas and agritourism, from glamorous and exclusive to cosy and friendly. You can also find many places where you can eat well and cheaply, such as tapas bars, pizzerias, restaurants and markets. You can also save money and time on transportation by using buses, taxis, ferries, bikes or cars.

Ibiza is a destination that will make you fall in love with

its beauty, culture and nightlife. The island will surprise you with its charm, creativity and energy. You will never get bored or tired of exploring its wonders and secrets. You will always find something new and exciting to do and see in Ibiza. You will always have an unforgettable holiday in Ibiza.

Printed in Great Britain
by Amazon

41791937R00145